Behavioural, Emotional
and Social Difficulties

Other books in the SEN in the Early Years Series
Coordinating Special Educational Needs –
    Damian Fitzgerald
Medical Conditions – Pam Dewis

Also available from Continuum
*Handbook of Social, Emotional and Behavioural
    Difficulties* – Morag Hunter-Carsch, Yonca Tiknaz,
    Rosemary Sage and Paul Cooper
Managing Behaviour in the Early Years – Janet Kay
100 Ideas for Managing Behaviour – Johnnie Young
Getting Your Little Darlings to Behave – Sue Cowley

Behavioural, Emotional and Social Difficulties

A Guide for the Early Years

Janet Kay

continuum

For Dan, who appears as himself, as always

Continuum International Publishing Group

The Tower Building   80 Maiden Lane, Suite 704
11 York Road   New York, NY 10038
SE1 7NX

www.continuumbooks.com

British Library Cataloguing-in-Publication Data
A catalogue record for this book is available from the British Library.
ISBN: 0826484697 (paperback)

Library of Congress Cataloging-in-Publication Data
A catalog record for this book is available from the Library of Congress.

Typeset by Fakenham Photosetting Limited, Fakenham, Norfolk
Printed and bound in Great Britain by Ashford Colour Press, Gosport, Hampshire

Contents

Introduction

There have been increasing levels of recognition and support for children with special educational needs (SEN) in recent years. A range of legislation and the introduction of the SEN Code of Practice (DfE1994, DfES 2001) have underpinned the development of specific support for children with learning difficulties across the range of educational provision. This development has been based on a set of principles that emphasize partnership with parents and children, and between agencies, as key factors in supporting effective service delivery to children with SEN and their families. Since 1998, the rapid increase in early years places for children aged 3 and 4 years old has meant that a much larger number of children with SEN are being identified at an earlier stage. Although early intervention is seen as a key factor for success in effectively supporting children with SEN, this development has placed considerable demands on settings, particularly non-maintained settings delivering the Foundation Stage.

Within the Code of Practice, four areas of learning difficulties are identified. However, although identified separately, it is acknowledged that these areas are interlinked. They are:

♦ communication and interaction

♦ cognition and learning

Behavioural, Emotional and Social Difficulties

♦ behaviour, emotional and social development

♦ sensory and/or physical development.
(DfES, 2001: 7: 52)

Medical conditions are also included, although it is made clear that a medical condition does not in itself mean that a child has SEN.
Within the Code of Practice, the term 'learning difficulty' is used to describe a 'special educational need' if a child:

♦ has a significantly greater difficulty in learning than the majority of children the same age

♦ has a disability that prevents or hinders her from making use of educational facilities of a kind generally provided for children of the same age, in schools within the area of the Local Authority (LA)

♦ is under compulsory school age and falls within either of the above, or will do so if special educational provision is not made for her.

This book is mainly concerned with behavioural, emotional and social difficulties (or social, emotional and behavioural difficulties – SEBD) that may affect learning and development, but it has to be recognized that for many children these categories are an artificial divide, useful for discussion and analysis but not necessarily reflecting individual children's real-life experiences.

Social, emotional and behavioural difficulties in context

At present around three per cent of all children in schools have statements of SEN and around 15 per cent of children have SEN without a statement. Sixty per cent of children with SEN are in mainstream schools. The number of children with SEN is increasing and is currently about 1.53 million, and between 0.2 and 1.07 per cent of pupils have statements for emotional and behavioural difficulties. Children with SEN are nine times more likely than children without SEN to be excluded from schools. Boys are twice as likely to have SEN without a statement. The figures indicate that more children are being identified as having SEN, they are more likely to be boys and they are also more likely to receive school meals, an indicator of relative poverty.

Children with SEBD are more likely to be excluded temporarily and permanently than other children, and are the central focus of concerns about disciplinary issues within settings. However, whereas other children with learning difficulties related to specific disorders are seen as neutral in the difficulties professionals face in supporting them, it continues to be a major struggle to implement policies that support children with SEBD without apportioning blame to them and assuming that their 'bad' behaviour is both consciously harmful and also within their power to control. One of the reasons for this may be that while many disabilities have more clear-cut or genetic causes, the development of SEBD is usually due to a complex interplay of factors relating to psychological, environmental and genetic factors. Environment, parenting and the child's own temperament may be contributing factors to the development of SEBD but the context within which the child's behaviour takes place, and responses of practitioners to that behaviour, quickly become part of the complex interplay of causal factors. As such, expectations about behaviour and responses to particular behaviours are part of the defining process by which children get the labels SEBD or EBD.

This book is aimed at early years practitioners, their managers, students and tutors on early years courses and parents interested in developing their understanding of SEN. In the context of this book, 'early years' will refer to children aged 0–8 years old in children's centres, nurseries, pre-schools, schools at home or the childminder's, and in any other setting where children spend time. 'Early years practitioner' refers to anyone working in these types of settings in any capacity and could include teachers, teaching assistants, nursery nurses, playworkers, pre-school workers and volunteers. 'Parent' refers to anyone with parental responsibility for a child.

Throughout the book the terms 'she' and 'he' are used randomly to avoid the more clumsy s/he and him/her.

1

Behavioural, Emotional and Social Development

In this chapter, children's social, emotional and behavioural development will be discussed with reference to early experience and typical development. The purpose of the chapter is to provide a basis for understanding the complex and diverse processes involved in children's development and to recognize the role of adults within this. It also seeks to acknowledge the links between a child's social and emotional development and consequent behavioural development.

To summarize, the chapter will help the reader achieve the following learning outcomes:

◆ understanding children's emotional, social and behavioural development and the links and interactions between these aspects

◆ understanding factors that influence development in these areas

◆ understanding the roles of parents and carers in children's emotional, social and behavioural development.

Early social behaviour and emotional attachment

Early social development takes place from birth onwards, with an amazingly rapid process of social learning taking place in the infant's first few weeks and months. This learning starts from the infant's first contact with others and includes making attachments to carers and significant others. The ability to make these early attachments successfully is vitally important to the infant's social relationships throughout childhood and later adult life. Social development is intricately linked with other forms of development, particularly cognitive and emotional. For example, a child needs the cognitive ability to 'place herself in the role of the other' to be able to express empathy, which is a significant factor in developing intimate relationships (Lewis 2002: 210).

Children's social development takes place in the context of their immediate and extended social networks, and it is the child's adaptation to these networks that is key. This process of adaptation is also linked to other aspects of development in that 'there is considerable evidence that many of the sensory and cognitive abilities of infants centre around making sense of their social environment' (Lewis 2002: 211).

Learning about social behaviour takes place over time and the starting point for this process is rooted in the innate survival mechanisms of newborn humans. Babies are born helpless in terms of their ability to survive independently, apart from some innate abilities that promote social interaction with carers. This mechanism is designed to ensure that adults will make a relationship with the child and care for and support the child. However, these innate abilities also set the foundation for the development of learned social behaviour in the child (Lewis 2002).

Some of these innate abilities relate to the baby's preferences in responses to different types of stimulation. It has been known for a while that 'the types of auditory and visual stimulation which adults provide are especially attractive to infants at or soon after birth' (Smith *et al.* 1998: 70). The types of stimulation that attract babies include human voices and faces.

It is not entirely agreed when responses to adult stimulation become evident in the child. There is a significant body of research which suggests that newborn infants seem to be attracted to faces, with some studies showing that newborns can recognize and show a preference for their mother at 2 days old (Ramsey and Langlois 2002). Other studies, however, suggest that newborns do not necessarily prefer human faces to other similar forms of stimulation. In the main it is agreed that by about 3 months babies are attracted to faces.

Recent research has shown that babies are particularly interested in making eye contact with others and that this ability is innate rather than learned. The research showed that babies as young as 2 days old can detect when someone is looking directly at them (Farroni *et al.* 2005). This study is important because eye contact is one of the most significant factors for building a foundation of social skills in infancy and beyond, and for making attachments with others.

Although the evidence suggests that newborn babies' initial social skills are innate, these form the basis of and are rapidly supplemented by social skills that are learned through interactions with others. For example, babies initially smile and cry as reflex reactions but learn the social nature of these behaviours when others respond to them. As the child learns about social responses to his behaviour, smiling and crying become learned behaviours rather than simple reflexes.

In addition, responsive interactions between the child and their carer seem to also be attractive to the child, with a particular preference for swift responses to the child's behaviour which may seem almost like a 'reply' (Smith *et al.* 1998). For example, when a mother rapidly responds to gurgling sounds from her baby by making similar sounds in return it almost seems like a 'conversation', as described in the case example below. This early development of social skills depends on carers involving themselves in interactions with the child and responding appropriately to the child's behaviour.

Marie and Gemma, 4 months old

Marie is sitting in the doctor's waiting room with Gemma, who is 4 months old, on her lap. Gemma is looking into her mother's face and smiling and making small gurgling noises. She waves her fists around and looks very alert and attentive. She seems filled with excitement and pleasure. Marie is looking into Gemma's face and they are making eye contact almost continually. Marie responds to the gurgling noises with similar noises and words

---

and her attention is completely on Gemma. They take turns to make soft noises to each other. Marie smiles and shakes her head at Gemma. Gemma responds by raising the volume of her gurgling and kicking her legs. Marie says 'look at you exercising' in a soft voice and Gemma chortles in response.

Most adults will respond to an infant with particular patterns of behaviour when interacting, such as smiles, wide-eyes, special voices and eye contact. However, it is when the adult and infant practice this interaction 'until the partners follow one another's lead smoothly and pleasurably' that attachment takes place (Bee 2000: 321). Over time, these responses between the carer and the child can become a smoothly choreographed interaction, and by about 6 or 7 months old the child will have differentiated between their main carer and others based on the quality and frequency of interactions.

This 'sensitivity' in response to the child's behaviour and needs is an important factor in attachment. It is also sometimes described as responsiveness and it depends on the carer being attuned to the child's needs.

Attachment and bonding are terms used to describe internal states. Bonds are affectionate relationships between any two specific individuals. Attachments are types of bonds on which the individual's security depends and these are characterized by the need for physical proximity and anxiety on separation (Bee 2000). Attachments are made to specific individuals and are enduring. In this sense, adults will bond with children as it is less likely that the adults' sense of security is bound up with the child, while children make attachments to their carers as part of their need to be protected and supported during their vulnerable infancy and childhood. Attachment is usually identified in infancy through observation of attachment behaviours in the carer and the child. Attachment takes place of around 6 months old and is characterized by the child showing a marked preference for a particular individual, usually, but not always, their main caregiver. This preference shows itself in different ways but involves protest at separation from the individual, more likelihood of being comforted by the individual, and more likelihood of smiling and interacting with the preferred person. Bowlby's early work on attachment theory focused on mother–child relationships almost exclusively, and for many infants, mothers are their first attachment figure. However, later evidence suggests that children can make their first attachment to one of a range of carers and significant others. The choice seems to depend on the quality, rather than the type, of interaction the carer has with the child.

From early infancy, young children are surrounded by a network of others, with whom they make relationships of a range of different types and intensities. Although the child's initial attachment has significance for future relationships these other relationships also have an important influence on the child's ongoing social development (Lewis 2002).

Jamie and George, 11 months old

Jamie is coming out of his house with his son, George, in his arms and with his friend Rob. On the path, Jamie remembers that he has left his wallet in the kitchen. He passes George to Rob and goes back into the house. George turns to look at Jamie as he walks away and stretches towards him, holding out his hand and leaning out of Rob's arms. He starts to grizzle and make little distressed noises. Rob speaks to him, saying 'don't worry he'll be back in a minute' and pats his back comfortingly, but George pulls away harder reaching towards the door and making louder distressed noises. Just as the door opens, George bursts into a loud roar and tears run down his face. Rob passes him back to Jamie and George immediately quietens and settles into his father's arms.

Early attachment is a key element in children's social development, providing the child with a blueprint for developing future relationships and a forum for learning about social interactions. The quality of a child's early attachments are significant in terms of their later social ability. However, not all children's early experiences of attachments may have the same quality. Ainsworth *et al.* (1978) identified a number of types of attachment in her well-known 'Strange Situation' experiments, following on from Bowlby's work in developing attachment theory. Ainsworth found different degrees of attachment between mother and child, which were placed in three categories representing different levels of security for the child. It seems clear from subsequent studies that while secure attachment is a predictive factor for positive social, emotional and behavioural development later on in childhood, insecure forms of attachment may indicate the opposite. Failures in attachment and insecure attachments may also be predictive factors for abuse and neglect in families.

Social behaviour beyond infancy

As the child grows older and more independent the child develops an 'internal working model' of her relationship with her primary attachment figure, which means that attachment becomes less dependent on physical proximity. This also means a decrease in some attachment behaviours such as separation anxiety. Internal working models can be defined as 'internal representations of the relationship in the child's mind' (Smith, Cowie and Blades 1998: 79). They are developed once the child has the cognitive ability to retain the concept of their attachment figure in his or her absence. Once a securely attached child has developed an internal working model, he may be able to spend more time away from his primary attachment figure, with less anxiety. Attachment behaviours such as proximity seeking and separation anxiety are still seen in children of 2 years old and above but tend to be more apparent in securely attached children when the child is tired, sick or distressed for some reason. A child with a less secure attachment may find separation more difficult and lack of confidence in primary attachments may therefore influence the child's development across the board. The insecurely attached child may find it hard to explore with confidence, make new relationships, or access learning opportunities and first-hand experiences success-fully. It is important to remember that although we see fewer attachment behaviours towards parents in children beyond infancy this does not mean that they are no longer attached. It usually means that the child has a good internal working model of their relationship, which provides the sources of support and comfort the child needs.

From the first significant attachment, infants will go on to make other attachments of differing strengths and importance with those around them. The extent to which children may successfully develop social skills will depend on their ability and the type of attachments they have experienced early on. The internal working model is a type of 'social script', which shapes the child's expectations of others, and his own behaviour, and also how the child views the behaviour of others (Bee 2000). The child will apply this early model to new relationships. As such, the quality of significant early relationships will have an impact on the child's social development and future relationships.

Securely attached children may have a better ability to make new social connections than those who are less securely attached. However, the majority of young children develop relationships with many others within and outside their families and these relationships all play a significant part in the child's social and other forms of development.

Engaging with peers and making friends

One key area of social development for children is with peers. Children start to be aware of other children from babyhood onwards but it is at the age of about 3 to 4 that children start to make reciprocal friendships with specific others. Children use and develop their existing social skills to make and maintain friendships with others. Children who are securely attached will have experience of patterns of interaction that are mutually rewarding and reciprocal, which they can use in making and developing new relationships.

The current emphasis on a play-based curriculum for 3–5 year olds is associated not just with learning through play, but with supporting children's social development and peer-relationships through frequent opportunities to interact. Social play involves a high level of reciprocity and cooperation to work well and children learn about turn-taking, sharing, allowing others to go first, controlling emotions and putting the continuity of the play before their own immediate needs or wishes. These are important skills for making and maintaining friendships, and children's initial ability to engage in social play is an important factor in their wider development.

Children who are rejected by peers may find it difficult to make friends and engage in play. They may fight and argue more, disrupt others' play and spend more time alone. Children who are rejected may have poorer social skills and a lower level of ability to respond appropriately to other children's behaviour (Smith, Cowie and Blades 1998). There is some evidence of links between poor relationships with peers in school and later problems with mental health, crime and dropping out of school.

Emotional development

Emotional development takes place intensively in the first years of life. Primary emotions such as happiness and unhappiness can be discerned in babies from very early on and children rapidly develop their ability to express their emotions in early infancy. Young children have developed most of the emotions they will experience by age 3.

Lewis (2002: 199) discusses the emergence of the 'primary or basic' emotions, which appear in the first 6–8 months of life. These are 'joy, sadness, disgust, anger, fearfulness and surprise'. These emotions are more basic because although the child experiences them, she is not conscious of this.

Children have usually established the ability to recognize themselves by 18 months and are using speech to describe emotions by the age of 2 years. Consciousness ('the ability to experience ourselves') usually comes between the ages of 2 and 3 (Lewis 2002: 200). Emotions such as empathy, jealousy and embarrassment emerge as children become aware of their own selves more. Other emotions develop when children are able to recognize and judge themselves against rules or standards and feel emotions in response to this such as pride, shame and embarrassment.

Babies can also recognize other's emotions from a very young age, responding to their caregiver's changing emotional expressions. This response develops into the use of social referencing, where the child 'checks out' his carer's response to a situation in order to formulate his own response.

Healthy emotional development is associated with children having their own emotional needs met from infancy.

Porter (2002: 191) argues that all children have these emotional needs:

♦ security: an assurance of protection and safety

♦ self-esteem: the need to value oneself

♦ autonomy: the need to be self-determining, to have some freedom

♦ belonging: the need to love and be loved and accepted.

A sense of security and belonging develops for children where they have secure loving relationships with parents and other carers and where their experiences outside the family are positive and reinforcing. Self-image is developed through the responses of significant others to the child. A child who experiences positive responses from parents and carers and who is given unconditional love and regard by those closest to her will develop a positive sense of self. This positive sense of self translates into good self-esteem, which means that the child places a high value on herself, based on the value others place on her. Autonomy or independence is important to children because in order to recognize themselves as competent, experimentation, mistakes and trying again are key factors in children's development of self-knowledge and self-esteem.

For some children, emotional difficulties may arise because disabilities may result in less adjusted emotional states. For other children, circumstances within their family and environment may mean that the child's emotional needs have not been met sufficiently for healthy emotional development to have taken place. The role of parents is significant in healthy emotional development and also in social and behavioural development.

Parenting styles and children's development

There is a substantial body of research that explores how different approaches to parenting may be influential in terms of children's development. One of the best-known models of parenting is Maccoby and Martin's (1983) which used two dimensions of parenting style. These were how demanding/undemanding parents were about the child's behaviour and how responsive/unresponsive parents were to the child. They described parenting styles in a four-fold classification (see the box below).

Maccoby and Martin's parenting models

Authoritative: high expectations of the child's behaviour and maturity, firm negotiated boundaries, good communication and high levels of warmth and responsiveness to the child's needs.

Authoritarian: high expectations of the child's behaviour and maturity, set boundaries and more severe disciplinary measures, poorer levels of responsiveness and communication.

Permissive: good communication, warmth and responsiveness, low expectations of behaviour and maturity, fewer and less consistent boundaries and disciplinary measures.

> **Neglecting/uninvolved**: poor levels of responsiveness and communication, low expectations of behaviour and maturity, lack of boundaries and controls.

The parenting style may vary according to the age and characteristics of each child in the family or may change over time according to changes in family composition and circumstances. However, parents are likely to have a predominant style of parenting which may be associated with one of the four models.

A number of studies have since supported the view that authoritative parenting, where responsiveness to the child's needs goes hand-in-hand with high expectations of maturity and behaviour is the most successful in terms of social outcomes for the child. Studies show that higher levels of popularity and good social skills were linked to authoritative parenting (Dekovic and Janssesns, 1992).

Mary, 3 years old

Mary leaves nursery tired and hungry after a hard day's play. She forgets her coat and when her mother asks her gently to go and fetch it Mary shouts 'No' at her. Mary's mother asks her again at which point, Mary hits her mother on the arm and shouts 'Go away' at her. Mary's mother picks her up and says quietly but very firmly, 'You are very tired so we will both get

---

the coat, but it is not OK to shout at me and hit.' Mary sobs a little on her mother's shoulder and then says 'Sorry Mummy.' They fetch the coat together and Mary puts it on quietly with her mother's help.

Authoritarian parenting has less positive outcomes with more likelihood of the child having more social difficulties, poorer educational outcomes and lower self-esteem. Authoritarian parents are less likely to negotiate with their children and more likely to be controlling and demanding of obedience.

Terri, 5 years old

Terri is shopping with her parents in a large out-of-town covered mall. They have been walking around the shops for four hours with one short break for a drink. Terri is bored, tired and thirsty and her legs are aching. She starts to get distressed, asking for a drink, to sit down or to go home. Her father tells her sharply to stop whining and that they will go home when he is ready. When Terri starts to cry she receives a slap on the bottom and is shouted at to be quiet and behave herself.

Permissive parenting is more likely to produce children who are less independent, more immature, more aggressive and who do less well in school.

James, 4 years old

James is running around in the park with his friends after school. He starts to play 'tag' with them but whenever he is 'on' he 'tags' the other children by hitting them hard on the back, laughing at them and shouting 'loser'. James' mother watches as she sits on a bench chatting to another parent but she does not intervene and when another parent points out James' behaviour to her she says 'He's alright, he's just playing.' After a short while the other children move away to their parents or in small groups and the game finishes.

Neglectful parenting usually has long-term effects on children's educational outcomes and social relationships, depending on the extent of the neglect. There is a relationship between poor or insecure attachment in early infancy and neglectful parenting. Children who are poorly attached and neglected are likely to have not had their emotional needs met sufficiently and may have problems in both social and emotional development.

Isaac, 6 years old

Isaac came to school today in dirty clothes and without having had any breakfast. His father did not get out of bed to see him off or help to prepare him for the school day. Isaac walked to school by himself, crossing two main roads and arriving very early. He is very thin and has not had a haircut for some time. Isaac doesn't say a lot at school and he tends to hang about on the edges of the playground football game. When he goes home, his father might still be in the pub and Isaac might have to let himself in with the key under the mat. He will look for food in the fridge and watch TV by himself. When his father gets home he may bring chips or not, but it is unlikely he will talk to Isaac about his school day or read with him before bedtime. Isaac doesn't have a bedtime but goes to bed when he has finished watching TV.

Influences on parenting

Studies into parenting style and developmental outcomes support the view that children's development is affected by parental behaviour and attitudes. However, parenting approaches do not develop independently but are often influenced by a range of factors. Belsky (1984) developed a model demonstrating the interactions between different influences on parenting. He found that the main influences are:

◆ the parent's own psychological resources (stability, ability to cope, own parenting and attachment experiences)

◆ the parent's social support (friends, family, community resources)

◆ the child's characteristics (temperament, health, intelligence).

Behavioural, Emotional and Social Difficulties

These factors can influence the extent to which parents can support their children, find time to communicate with them, show warmth and respond to their needs. For example, parents who have had poor parenting themselves may find it more difficult to show warmth, or recognize and respond to their children's needs. There is also evidence that mothers who suffer from depression may be more neglecting as they are less responsive and less aware of their children's needs.

One of the important issues Belsky recognizes is that children are not passive in the parenting process. The child's personality and behaviour, birth order, health and other characteristics will have an influence on how the parent responds to them. This may be why children in the same family may have different parenting experiences. The child's temperament, such as an irritable baby, may affect how the parent responds to them but there is evidence that this may only be a significant negative factor if the parent also has low levels of support and lacks stability. The parent's own experiences of parenting and attachment, their childhood experiences, education and social situation are also very influential. Parents who have good family and social support networks are likely to develop more positive parenting styles, as are parents with better educational qualifications and family relationships.

Environmental factors are significant in influencing both parenting style and the child's direct experiences. Key environmental factors are poverty, work, community resources, availability of quality childcare and education and social support networks. Bronfenbrenner (1979) developed an ecological systems model showing how these and other factors interact to determine the child's experience and influence the parent's behaviour. For example, a parent who is struggling with poverty may be more distant and anxious, less tolerant and more stressed. Poverty may also mean a less safe neighbourhood and poorer quality housing. It may mean that a parent has to work long hours or may be unemployed and possibly suffering depression. The parent may have less time to play and communicate with the child. There may be fewer social and community resources available and less access to good quality care and education. However, environmental factors alone do not determine parenting style.

Many families in poverty parent successfully, despite the difficulties they may face with lack of resources. It is the combination of personal coping skills, levels of support and environment that will determine parenting approach. These factors can also change over time and according to life events. For example, divorce, bereavement, the loss of a job or the start of a new job, the birth of a baby into the family or moving to a new community may all impact, at least temporarily, on parenting style. There is evidence, for example, that newly divorced parents may use less positive parenting styles for a period of time.

Behavioural development

The extent to which emotional needs are met by parents and social development is successful will be key determinants of a child's behaviour. As such, one of the main factors in most children's behavioural development is the relationship the child has with her parents from birth onwards. There are some children, however, where behavioural development is also affected by specific conditions or disabilities. These will be discussed in Chapter 2.

Some significant environmental factors affecting behavioural development are:

♦ family type and composition

♦ the family's social and cultural background

♦ home setting and environment

♦ parenting styles and child-rearing practices

♦ relationships with parents, siblings and other family members

♦ the family's employment and financial situation

♦ support for learning and other aspects of development in the home

♦ the child's own emotional needs and the extent to which these are met

♦ the child's social skills and ability to relate to peers and adults

♦ any disabilities which may influence the child's developmental progress

♦ factors influencing family behaviour e.g. illness, loss of jobs, bereavement, separation and divorce. (Kay 2006: 37–8)

These factors interact to determine the child's behaviour, creating a complex matrix of influences which impact on each child in a unique way, depending on the child's own character and temperament and level of resilience to stress.

Authoritative parenting approaches have the most positive outcomes for children's behavioural development 'in terms of mature behaviour, good social skills, emotional stability and self-control, and effective learning skills' (Kay 2006: 54). Key factors in behavioural development are the disciplinary measures used by parents and the extent to which parents monitor and manage their children and show them warmth (Patterson 1996; Patterson *et al.* 1989 cited in Bee 2000: 11).

One of Patterson's findings was that once behavioural problems are established they can become compounded because they lead to problems in other areas of the child's life, such as achievement in school and friendship. This may lead to further behavioural problems for the child, especially where aggressive behaviour leads to rejection by other children.

Behavioural development is also affected by context in the sense that behavioural expectations may vary considerably over time and between different families, communities and cultures. There is no single standard for behaviour and children's behaviour may be judged differently at home in comparison to another setting. Views on a child's behaviour will often have a subjective element to them, which may affect how a child is seen in a particular context. For example, behaviour will vary greatly in a group of 3 year olds in a nursery setting, depending on age and stage of development, maturity, social experience and social skills, levels of distress and the extent to which emotional needs are being met and relationships with significant adults have formed. This is significant in terms of 'labelling' which may determine a child's ongoing behaviour by signifying that the child is badly behaved and therefore perpetuating this behaviour. This is discussed further in Chapter 2.

Conclusion

In this chapter, children's social, emotional and behavioural development has been discussed, with reference to some of the environmental and parenting influences on development. In the next chapter, developmental issues that may lead to behaviour, social and emotional SEN will be discussed, including disabilities and developmental differences.

2

Behavioural, Emotional and Social Difficulties

In this chapter, some of the issues and difficulties children may experience in their behavioural, social and emotional development will be discussed along with an exploration of some of the reasons why these may arise.

To summarize, this chapter will help the reader to achieve the following learning outcomes:

♦ understand the range of issues and difficulties children may experience in their social, emotional and behavioural development

♦ understand some of the reasons why these difficulties may arise

♦ recognize that behavioural difficulties need to be viewed within the social context, for example the school or home

♦ recognize the relationship between social, emotional and behavioural issues and a range of learning difficulties, disabilities and more complex needs.

Behavioural, Emotional and Social Difficulties

Behavioural, emotional and social difficulties can be defined in a myriad of different ways, but for the purposes of this book the definition used will be drawn from the SEN Code of Practice. Children with learning difficulties relating to behavioural, social and emotional development are defined within the Code of Practice as:

> Children and young people who demonstrate features of emotional and behavioural difficulties, who are withdrawn and isolated, disruptive and disturbing, hyperactive and lack concentration; those with immature social skills; and those presenting challenging behaviours arising from other complex special needs may require help or counselling for some, or all, of the following:
>
> ♦ flexible teaching arrangements
>
> ♦ help with development of social competence and emotional maturity
>
> ♦ help in adjusting to school expectations and routines
>
> ♦ help in acquiring the skills of positive interaction with peers and adults
>
> ♦ specialized behavioural and cognitive approaches
>
> ♦ re-channelling or re-focusing to diminish repetitive or self-injurious behaviours
>
> ♦ provision of class or school systems which control or censure negative or difficult behaviours and encourage positive behaviour
>
> ♦ provision of a safe and supportive environment. (DfES 2001: 7: 60)

Behavioural, Emotional and Social Difficulties

The terms 'learning difficulties' and 'special educational needs' are defined in the introduction. In addition, the terms emotional and behavioural difficulty (EBD) and social, emotional and behavioural difficulty (SEBD) are used regularly in the literature in this area and will also be used in this book. EBD is described in the Code of Practice as:

> Evidence of significant emotional or behavioural difficulties, as indicated by clear recorded examples of withdrawn or disruptive behaviour; a marked and persistent inability to concentrate; signs that the child experiences considerable frustration or distress in relation to their learning difficulties; difficulties in establishing and maintaining balanced relationships with their fellow pupils or with adults; and any other evidence of a significant delay in the development of life and social skills. (DfES 2001: 7: 43)

It is clear that the SEN category 'behavioural, emotional and social development' covers a wide range of needs and requirements, and that there are many different reasons why children may experience learning difficulties related to these areas. For example, behavioural difficulties that are central to, or a complicating factor in, a child's learning difficulties may arise from disabilities such as attention deficit and hyperactivity disorder (ADHD) or they may be the result of emotional difficulties arising from early neglect or abuse or other deficits in the child's early environment and parenting experiences.

Jones (2005) gives a helpful distinction between 'impairment' and 'disability' by defining 'impairment' as something that exists within the child (which could be physical, emotional, sensory or cognitive), for example autism. Disability, on the other hand, is the way in which the impairment affects the child's ability to function effectively within the social context. As such, the extent of disability can be affected by factors external to the child, such as attitudes of others, availability of relevant services, knowledge and under-standing of how specific impairments affect children, and knowledge about the most effective ways of supporting children with impairments in a range of contexts. For example, Dan has severe dyslexia. In classes at school where the teaching and learning focuses on his knowledge and understanding of the subject, where he can use his considerable oral skills effectively, and where literacy is not the key basis for judgements about ability, or where he has a reader/writer, Dan is a committed, able pupil who contributes to his own and others' learning. In other classes where he is judged more by his ability to read and record, he is much less able, contributes much less and is less committed. Dan's impairment is his dyslexia, but he is more or less disabled at different times depending on how teaching and learning is structured and differen-tiated for him within his school setting, and what sort of support he gets to acquire and use literacy skills.

There are many interacting factors which may lead to emotional, behavioural and social difficulties, but it is important to remind ourselves that there is not a single causal link to any one factor. For example, not all children living in poverty develop SEBD, but children living in socially deprived areas are over-represented among those with SEBD. Other significant factors are:

♦ gender and ethnicity

♦ learning difficulties or other disabilities

♦ language development delays

♦ poor-quality parenting

♦ loss, bereavement or trauma

♦ abuse and/or neglect.

Factors associated with parenting have been discussed in Chapter 1. Some of the other factors are discussed in more detail in this chapter.

It is important to remember that, while behavioural, emotional and social difficulties, and issues relating to these, are discussed separately at times within this chapter, there are significant links between deficits in emotional and social development and behavioural problems. In addition, there can be strong negative reinforcing effects between these factors, for example, when behavioural problems may lead to a child becoming more socially isolated and less emotionally stable, leading to further behavioural difficulties.

Gender and ethnicity

One of the key determinants of SEBD is gender. Boys are more likely to have severe or mild learning difficulties than girls in ratios 1.2:1 and 1.6:1. Boys are also three times more likely to have autistic spectrum disorders (ASD) with learning difficulties than girls. While 7.6 per cent of girls aged 5–15 years have mental health problems, the figure for boys is 11.4 per cent. Nearly half of boys in public care have mental health problems, while the figure for girls is 39 per cent. Boys are also twice as likely to have dyslexia than girls and 2.3:1 more boys than girls are diagnosed with ADHD. Overall, boys are twice as likely to have learning difficulties than girls and are much more likely to be identified as having SEBD whether they are statemented or not.

The reasons for gender differences in SEBD are complex and remain unclear. Various different theories – biological, social and organizational – have been suggested, with no single or simple cause identified. Boys are more likely to have genetic disorders such as Fragile X syndrome, which affects learning and behaviour, and boys are also more likely to have ASD, which leads to speculation about boys being more vulnerable to developmental problems. However, there may also be differences in diagnoses of girls and boys, with behavioural problems driving diagnoses such as ADHD in boys, and possibly being less noticeable in girls due to differences in socialization and gender expectations. Another suggestion is that boys are more likely to react adversely to social problems, particularly family breakdown, which often involves less contact with fathers.

Ethnicity is also a factor in a child's chances of being diagnosed as having learning difficulties, but the picture is complex and there are many factors involved. For example, there is a high number of children from South Asian backgrounds in the UK who have learning difficulties, many of which are linked to high levels of poverty and social deprivation. People aged 5–32 years from South Asian communities are three times more likely to have learning difficulties than white people. South Asian families suffer 'simultaneous disadvantage' from poverty, racism and discrimination, and inequalities in access to employment, housing and social and health services. South Asian families may also be disadvantaged by stereotypical expectations about their behaviour, for example, that their communities are self-contained and 'look after their own' and therefore do not require services. The result is higher levels of mild and moderate learning difficulties among South Asian children, which are linked to their socio-economic background (Mir *et al.* 2001). Pakistani children are also more likely to have multiple and profound learning difficulties and sensory impairments, which may possibly be attributed to genetic factors associated with close blood relatives marrying (consanguinity). However, Asian and Chinese children are less likely to be identified as having moderate and specific learning difficulties or ASD. It is possible that this may be due to difficulties in untangling the effects of English as an additional language (EAL) and learning difficulties in young children, leading to under-identification for this population.

Black Caribbean and White/Black Caribbean children are 1.5 times more likely to be identified as having SEBD than white children. This may be due to racism and differential expectations and treatment of black children in schools. Discrimination and associated factors may also affect outcomes for traveller children. One of the findings of the DfES Research Report on SEN and ethnicity was that ethnic variations were more likely where social and contextual factors were significant in the development of learning difficulties (such as SEBD), as opposed to learning difficulties more attributable to physiological reasons (such as sensory impairments). Therefore, some ethnic minority children who are more likely than white children to be subject to poorer environments and discrimination may be over-represented as having SEBD (Lindsay *et al.* 2006).

Learning disabilities and difficulties and mental health problems

There are many reasons why children have or develop learning disabilities or difficulties. These may be due to genetic factors, developmental factors or brain damage. As such, learning diffi-culties may be the result of specific disabilities or may be due to early experiences for example, abuse and neglect. Research into brain development in infants tells us that social experiences and the child's interactions with the environment in infancy have a significant impact on brain development and cognitive functioning. Poor-quality experiences, lack of attachment, low levels of stimulation and neglect can result in lack of development of the child's cognitive ability in infancy, which may impact negatively on learning.

About 25/1000 children have mild/moderate learning difficulties and in the UK there are about 65,000 children with severe learning difficulties (DfES 2006b). Overall, 1/20 children have learning difficulties in the broadest sense. Learning difficulties may be general, affecting all aspects of learning, or specific, for example dyslexia which affects mainly literacy skill development. Learning difficulties may be temporary or long-term and some may decrease in response to a supportive environment, whereas others may have long-term permanent effects for the child's cognitive development. Learning can be affected by cognitive impairments or social and emotional issues, or a complex combination of these factors.

There are patterns to learning difficulties associated with socioeconomic and family background. Mild learning difficulties are more common among children from poorer backgrounds or adverse family situations. There is a link between poverty and learning difficulties, possibly due to increased childcare costs and fewer opportunities for parents to work due to the child's care requirements.

Children with learning difficulties are more likely to have mental health problems. This may be due to adverse social situations such as rejection by peers, failure to make social relationships, feelings of isolation and failure, or difficult life events associated with having learning difficulties. However, there is also a link between mental health problems in children and poverty and family conflict. Ten per cent of all children aged 5–15 years have mental health problems (MIND 2006). While problems such as schizophrenia are more often identified in adolescence, emotional disorders, hyperactivity and conduct disorders (behavioural problems) are increasingly being identified in young children. There are higher rates of mental health problems among children who come from single-parent families, step-families, and large families with more than five children. Mental health problems are also elevated in families with low incomes, poor parental educational qualifications and/or unemployment. In families where parents have mental health problems, children have an increased chance of developing mental health problems themselves.

Behavioural problems and learning difficulties

Behavioural problems in children have become more noticeable in the early years as more young children enter pre-school settings. For some of these children, behavioural problems will recede and they will not experience ongoing difficulties with their learning development. However, there is also evidence that for some children behavioural problems in the early years are an indicator for more severe or persistent behavioural difficulties in older primary and secondary school children. It seems that for a significant proportion of children, the earlier that behavioural problems start, the more problematical they will become as the child grows older (Moffit 1993; Pierce, *et al.* 1999).

While children with behavioural problems are less likely to be able to successfully access the curriculum, children with learning difficulties are more likely to develop behavioural problems (Foot *et al.* 2004). There are well-documented links between a poor development of literacy skills and behaviour problems, and also between social and language development and behavioural problems, which are discussed in more detail below.

All children display behavioural challenges at times. For many children these relate to life events, such as significant transitions like going to nursery or starting school. Other children may respond to changes at home with some behavioural challenges, for example, in response to the birth of a new baby in the family or becoming part of a step-family. Some stages of development result in more demanding behaviour in many children, hence the well-documented struggle for independence many 2–3 year olds go through. These behavioural challenges are common to most children and are generally seen as part of development and growth towards maturity. With support and sensitive handling on the part of parents and early years practitioners, most children pass through phases or periods of difficult behaviour and move to a more mature stage of development.

However, for some children, difficulties are a much more persistent aspect of behaviour, and improvements in behavioural development are slow and hard to achieve. For these children, behavioural difficulties may have a significant and very negative impact on cognitive and social development. They may affect the way that adults and peers relate to the child; they may influence the extent to which the child can access learning opportunities; and they may be strongly linked to emotional distress.

Most difficult behaviour is reactive – a response to a particular situation so the child's behaviour is not taking place in a vacuum but is a part of the child's interaction with a specific context. We need to view the child's behaviour not just as an intrinsic part of the child, but as a dynamic process between the child and the environment.

Behavioural difficulties may lead to learning difficulties in cases where the child's behaviour persistently impedes his ability to access the curriculum within an early years setting or to develop social skills and make positive relationships with peers and adults. Behavioural difficulties may include a wide range of different persistent behaviours such as:

◆ disruption of routines, play or other learning experiences

◆ verbal or physical aggression towards peers or adults

◆ inability to concentrate or engage with learning experiences

◆ distraction of self or others

◆ refusal to engage in learning activities or respond to requests

◆ destructive behaviour, e.g. breaking toys or damaging the environment

◆ bizarre behaviour, e.g. making strange faces or noises in an inappropriate situation

◆ withdrawn behaviour, e.g. curling in a foetal position, refusing to talk or respond to conversation, isolation.

Conversely, learning difficulties may lead to behavioural problems where a child struggling to access learning may become bored and frustrated, developing feelings of anxiety and failure and possibly losing confidence and gaining a less positive self-image.

Learning difficulties may result in some of the following behaviours:

- frustration, anger and distress with the learning process

- challenging behaviour designed to distract from the learning process

- refusal to be involved in learning activities

- non-compliance

- aggression, attention-seeking behaviour and distraction of other children from the task at hand

- poor concentration, restlessness and lack of application

- low self-esteem, problems with peers, social exclusion. (Kay 2006: 83)

The key issue is that children may have learning difficulties for a wide range of reasons, however, it is the difficulties a child experiences in the learning environment which may lead to behavioural problems. For some children with specific disabilities that may involve particular patterns of behaviour, for example obsessive or repetitive behaviour, the mis-match between expectations in the setting and the child's response may be acutely obvious.

Roffey (2004: 97) uses the following categories to identify children with both behavioural problems and learning difficulties:

- They are developing at a slower pace than others.

- They have a specific difficulty, especially in literacy

skills, where they consistently fail to meet the expectations of others.

♦ They do not understand the language of instruction.

♦ They have unmet emotional needs or are experiencing great distress which impinges on their ability to learn.

♦ They are not skilled in paying attention to teacher input and have fragmented concentration on set tasks.

♦ They are more able than their peers and either are trying to 'fit in' or are under-stimulated in class.

However, it is important to remember that for many children these categories may overlap and lead to compound social and emotional problems as well.

Dan

Dan started reception class at the age of 4 and a half. At this stage, Dan's severe dyslexia was just starting to be identified and it was unclear as to whether he had a specific or more general learning difficulty. Over the next two years Dan struggled with all aspects of literacy learning and quickly became adept at avoiding engagement with any aspect of literacy apart from being read to, which he loved. However, Dan also became very anxious about this and tried hard to hide the fact that he was not able to make the same

---

progress in literacy as other children. The difficulties Dan had, and his need to conceal these to maintain self-esteem, made him feel isolated and 'different' from other children. As his social acceptance wavered, Dan resorted to loud and sometimes disruptive playground behaviour to get the attention of peers. Other children sometimes avoided Dan because of this and he came to feel isolated and worried about having few friends. This, in turn, lowered Dan's self-esteem further, and he became very resistant to trying new things or risking making a mistake. His avoidance of literacy learning became very sophisticated. In class, Dan said nothing and he clearly did not feel able to contribute to discussion. He described himself as 'rubbish' at school and became a lonely, sad and angry little boy for a time.

Disabilities

Children with certain disabilities may be more vulnerable to emotional, social and behavioural problems than other children. This does not mean that having a specific disability automatically means a child will have SEBD. However, if the child's disability makes it difficult for her to cope with the learning environment and the support available is insufficient to help the child cope, emotional, social and behavioural issues may arise. Currently, there are about 700,000 children with disabilities in Britain (MIND 2006).

Schopler (1995) used the analogy of an iceberg to demonstrate the relationship between behavioural problems and impairments experienced by children with autism. The child's behaviour is the visible part of the 'iceberg' but underneath are the many factors influencing that behaviour. For example, in a situation where a child with poor understanding of expectations in the learning environment is under pressure to conform to standards that she cannot understand, her behaviour will be the outward manifestation of the tension between these factors.

As such, the extent to which impairments may lead to difficult behaviour will depend on:

♦ the type and severity of the impairments

♦ the extent to which these are understood and responded to effectively by key adults at home and in the setting

♦ the extent to which the learning environment has been adapted to meet the child's needs

♦ the effectiveness of support for the child's social integration and emotional development.

The range of disabilities that may affect children's learning and behaviour is too wide for us to look at in detail here, however, a small number of disabilities that commonly lead to learning difficulties are discussed below as examples. It is important to remember that the disability is not the only determinant of the child's learning and behavioural issues, but that the interface between the child's impairments and the child's environment will also be a significant factor.

Activity

With reference to a child you know who has a learning disability and behavioural problems, write down the issues the child faces:

♦ accessing learning opportunities

♦ developing social skills, making friends and integrating with the group

♦ maintaining emotional stability.

Then write down the resources the child has access to cope with these challenges:

♦ in the setting

♦ at home

♦ from other sources

♦ from self.

Draw an 'iceberg' model showing the child's behaviour and the factors that underpin this, adding in what may help and support the child and any other factors which may negatively affect the child's behaviour.

What changes could be made to the child's inter-action with adults and the learning environment to better support his/her behavioural development?

Autistic spectrum disorders (ASD)

Autism is not a single disability but a range of conditions commonly known as ASD, which vary considerably in terms of the impact on the child's emotional, social and cognitive functioning. Children with severe ASD may be more likely to be in special schools but there are many children with milder forms of ASD in mainstream school. About 1/200 children have ASD. Some forms of ASD are not necessarily automatically associated with learning difficulties, such as Asperger syndrome. However, children with ASD who have reasonable cognitive functioning may still develop learning difficulties associated with SEBD.

There are three common areas of impairment currently used to identify ASD:

♦ social interaction (failure to understand social cues or non-verbal communication, socially unresponsive, lack of interest in others, difficulty making friendships)

♦ communication (poor language skills, literal interpretation of language, repetitive language use)

♦ imagination (narrow range of activities and interests, repetitive play or behaviour).

However, a recent study has suggested that autism may have more complex effects than the three areas of impairment traditionally cited, and that it may be a global disorder affecting how the brain processes information, rather than just the social disorder it has been considered to be to date. Williams *et al.* (2006) found that children with autism have impairments to a wider range of brain functions than previously thought. They found that autistic children in their study, who were all literate and able to speak, had difficulties with any complex tasks and problems with balance, movement, memory and sensory perception. The researchers suggest that these problems may be due to abnormalities in the ways in which the different sections of the brain communicate, making it difficult for areas of the brain controlling different functions to work together.

The average age of diagnosis is 5 years old, and boys are four times more likely than girls to have ASD. Learning difficulties arise from ASD for a number of reasons. Some children may never develop language and communication skills, others may have impaired language ability, poor understanding of social cues and responses and/or be socially unresponsive. In addition to the difficulties this creates for the child in successfully accessing the curriculum, there is also a strong link between EBD and language difficulties, as discussed in the next section.

Children with ASD may have significant difficulties in making friendships and relating to others. They may find aspects of the setting emotionally stressful such as requirements to behave in certain ways according to rules and group demands. They may not understand requests or instructions easily and they may find interactions with others incomprehensible or threatening. One area where children with ASD usually have problems is play. Impairments to imagination which are a feature of

ASD include lack of ability to use imagination in 'pretend' play, a limited range of play behaviours, repetitive behaviour and a narrow range of interests and activities. Linked to poor social interaction this may lead to social exclusion in the group and lack of opportunity to develop social and learning skills through play and interaction with others.

Behavioural problems in children with ASD may vary considerably or not be present. However, they may include:

♦ non-communication

♦ outbursts, over-reaction to incidents

♦ non-compliance with requests

♦ physical withdrawal, refusal to engage or join in

♦ inappropriate, rude comments or behaviour

♦ repetitive, obsessional behaviours.

Behavioural issues may arise as part of the child's disability or may be a response to environmental pressures or failure to comprehend expectations.

Attention deficit and hyperactivity disorder (ADHD)

This condition is usually diagnosed early in childhood and usually involves:

♦ lack of concentration

♦ impulsive behaviour

♦ inability to settle or sit still

♦ lack of self-confidence

♦ disruptive and/or destructive behaviour.

Key factors are hyperactivity and lack of attention. Some children are described as having ADD as they are inattentive but not hyperactive. ADHD and ADD affect learning because concentration problems, poor self-organization and inability to follow instructions may affect access to the curriculum. Children with ADHD and ADD also often have problems with making and sustaining relationships due to poor self-control of behaviour, unstable emotional states, and sometimes physical and verbally aggressive behaviour. It is common for children with ADHD to become socially isolated which may compound emotional distress and enhance the child's learning difficulties. Children with ADHD and ADD are often labelled as having SEBD because their complex range of social, emotional and behavioural difficulties can compound each other and intensify the child's learning difficulties.

Language and communication development

Benner *et al.* (2002) found that about three-quarters of children with emotional and behavioural difficulties also have language problems, and half of children with language problems have behavioural and emotional issues. Children with anti-social behaviour were ten times more likely to have language problems than other children. In early years settings, children with poor language and social skills and limited levels of concentration are more likely to develop behavioural problems (Ofsted 2005).

Language problems may be a result of a particular disability such as ASD or may be the result of poor parental care and lack of stimulation in the home. Children with English as an additional language (EAL) may struggle with lack of a common language with peers and practitioners but this usually resolves as the child acquires English, unless there is insufficient support or the child has other difficulties that may compound her communication problems.

A key factor in the link between language difficulties and behavioural disorders is the difficulties the child has in initiating and sustaining social relationships. Language is a key tool for children in regulating their own behaviour. As self-control develops at age 3–4 years, language becomes a tool in this, developing into internal speech at 6–7 years, which allows the child to reason, problem-solve and reflect, and develop rule-governed behaviour. These are key skills for developing social relationships with peers and adults. Children with language difficulties may have problems managing their own behaviour in relation to others and may not be able to develop friendship or become integrated in the group.

Other factors are difficulties in joining in class activities, understanding the language of instruction, responding to questions and acquiring literacy skills.

Emotional and social development and behaviour

Some of the factors in a child's immediate family and community environment which may impact on development have been discussed in Chapter 1. There is a well-documented link between poor environment, less positive parenting approaches, and children's behavioural and emotional problems. Laever's (2003) work on involvement in learning and emotional well-being links these factors, arguing that children cannot learn as successfully unless their emotional well-being has been assured. As such, emotional distress can significantly impair children's ability to access the curriculum. Other studies also support the view that children need to be emotionally stable in order to learn effectively and make good social relationships.

All children experience positive and negative emotions and turbulent, unstable emotional states at times. Particular stages of development may be more emotionally difficult than others, for example, many toddlers go through difficult emotional states as they struggle towards mastering their emotions and recognizing the needs of others. Transitions of any sort can be emotionally difficult, for example starting nursery, moving up to school, moving house and any changes in family composition. However, children also have different abilities to deal with and resolve emotional difficulties, based on their character and experiences. The majority of emotional difficulties for children are short lived and with time and sensitive handling can be overcome if the child has a normally stable emotional state. However, some children experience more acute, ongoing emotional difficulties that may affect their learning and social development more acutely and over a longer period of time.

Emotional difficulties may be the root of behavioural problems and/or result from these. Emotional issues may be linked to other learning difficulties or disabilities and/or the child's problems in accessing the curriculum or social acceptance in the setting. Some emotional difficulties may be the result of difficult experiences such as illness, abuse or neglect, or traumatic experiences in the child's early environment.

Emotional difficulties may also result in behavioural, social and learning difficulties such as:

♦ difficulty in dealing with new situations, individuals or experiences

♦ reluctance to experiment, take risks or accept challenges

♦ slower learning or more difficulties in learning

♦ inability to problem-solve effectively

♦ easily distressed, over-sensitive and unable to handle criticism

♦ social isolation, difficulty in making friends, frequent conflict with others.

Social difficulties may be closely linked to emotional difficulties and/or may be one of the problems arising from other conditions or disabilities as discussed above. A child may have social difficulties if he is diagnosed as being on the autistic spectrum as social difficulties are part of this condition. Another child may have social difficulties because of behavioural problems, which isolate her from others and discourage others from involving her in play or other activities. All children with learning difficulties are vulnerable to social isolation. Social difficulties can also be an issue for children with low self-esteem or those with medical conditions that result in long absences from the educational setting. Examples of social problems are:

♦ social isolation, lack of friends, poor relationships with peers

♦ bullying, being bullied

♦ social immaturity, different social behaviour to peers

♦ inability to communicate effectively with others

♦ inability to share, negotiate and cooperate in play and other activities.

The impact of abuse and neglect

NSPCC (2006) research shows that:

♦ Seven per cent of children experienced serious physical abuse.

♦ One per cent of children experienced sexual abuse by a parent or carer and another three per cent by another relative. Eleven per cent of children experienced sexual abuse by people known but unrelated to them. Five per cent of children experienced sexual abuse by an adult stranger or someone they had just met.

♦ Six per cent of children experienced serious absence of care at home.

Behavioural, Emotional and Social Difficulties

◆ Six per cent of children experienced frequent and severe emotional maltreatment.

◆ Sixteen per cent of children experienced serious maltreatment by parents, of whom one third experienced more than one type of maltreatment.

◆ Latest available figures show that there are 32,700 children on child protection registers in the UK at 31 March 2003.

This last figure represents just the proportion of children who are actually identified as being abused by the authorities. There is evidence that the actual figure may be much higher and that a significant proportion of abuse may never come to light.

All forms of abuse can lead to emotional damage in children. The failure of parents to make effective attachments to their children; persistent denial of the child's rights to safety and security; feelings of self-blame and low self-esteem and lack of a sense of belongingness can significantly harm healthy emotional development throughout childhood. Sexually abused children may develop the belief that they are only valued as sexual beings for the gratification of others and not valued for themselves. This may lead to self-loathing and self-harming, angry or withdrawn behaviour and inability to make positive relationships. For many abused children, the long-term emotional damage is the most significant negative effect of the abuse, as it may result in low self-esteem, poor relationships, drug and alcohol abuse and poor life chances and life choices.

Children who experience abuse have much higher rates of mental health problems, including stress, anxiety, depression, personality disorders and increased levels of self-harm and suicidal behaviour.

There are approximately 61,100 children in public care in England, many of whom have suffered abuse and/or neglect. Many abused children and other children who spend part or all of their childhood in the public care system achieve outcomes in terms of qualifications, employment, successful relationships and mental health which are all still much poorer than those of other children. For example, only 30 per cent of school leavers who are in public care gain one or more GCSEs or equivalent, and 1 in 4 children in care aged 14 are not in school. In addition,

45 per cent of young people aged between 5 and 17 looked after by local authorities in England were assessed as having a mental disorder. 5–10 year olds were about 5 times more likely to have a mental disorder than children living in private households (42 per cent compared with 8 per cent).' (DfES 2006c)

Eleven per cent of children in public care have emotional problems compared to two per cent of other children; 36 per cent have conduct disorders compared to five per cent of others; and 11 per cent have hyperactivity compared to two per cent of other children (MIND 2006). Overall, 49 per cent of boys and 39 per cent of girls in care have mental health problems. In the past, the focus on securing children's welfare in terms of ending abuse and neglect has meant less attention to other aspects of development, with educational disruptions and poor monitoring of health development being common for many children in the care system.

However, since the Utting Report (1997) highlighted the appalling outcomes for children in care, the Quality Protects initiative introduced in 1998 has sought to improve educational and health outcomes for children in care through target setting and close monitoring of individual children. A major factor, however, is the stability of the child's placement in care. Mental health problems are significantly reduced in children in care who have stable placements. The reality for many children is, sadly, that placements are not stable and the child is continually moving between foster homes until a vicious circle develops as the child's emotional and behavioural states deteriorate, triggering further placement breakdowns.

The incidence of mental disorders in primary school-aged children in care reflects a complex negative pattern of events for some children, which compound each other to significantly damage emotional development and impair mental health. These may include:

♦ poor attachment and negative patterns of parenting

♦ abuse and/or neglect

♦ separation from family members, including some or all siblings

♦ disrupted education and/or care placements

♦ at least one (and for some children many more) change of carer

♦ loss of contact with or access to significant people and places

- difficulties making new attachments to new carers

- learning delays and difficulties

- behavioural problems.

Without effective support and help, these problems may continue through later childhood, adolescence and into adulthood.

Helena, 5 years old

Helena, 5, lived with her single mother, who is a heroin addict, until she was 4 years old. Life with her mother was chaotic and parenting was extremely inconsistent and lacking in emotional warmth. Helena was made the subject of a Care Order at age 4 because of neglect and physical abuse, and she was then placed with foster carers. Helena is very confused by the changes that have happened to her and frequently displays a great deal of hostility and anger to those around her. She is destructive and unable to control her angry impulses. She hits out, screams and uses aggressive language with adults and peers. On other occasions, Helena can be withdrawn and sad, unresponsive to efforts to engage her or communicate in any way. Helena has been referred to children's therapeutic services for assessment because of concerns that she may have significant difficulties making attachments to others.

Labelling children with emotional and behavioural difficulties

In the introduction to this book, it is mentioned that children with SEBD are more likely to be excluded from schools than other children and that there is often a different attitude towards children when behavioural issues are at the heart of SEN than when SEN is linked to other types of disabilities. There is a covert belief system in some educational settings that behaviour can be controlled and changed by the child and a blame culture attached to children who continue to behave in unwanted ways. This links to dominant views of behaviour management, which rely heavily on reward and punishment, as opposed to approaches which recognize behaviour as an aspect of development (Kay 2006).

In order to understand more about how children become labelled as having 'challenging behaviour' it is important to understand the processes that take place between children and their environments. The concept of 'challenging behaviour' is very subjective, depending on the views of the practitioner applying this label and the context within which the behaviour takes place. As such, in order to consider behavioural aspects of SEN, the behaviour needs to be viewed within the context in which it is taking place. Hargraves *et al.* (1975) suggested that 'behaviour in context' is a concept that recognizes that the child's actions (or behaviour) will be viewed as problematical or non-problematical depending on person, place and timing. This concept is useful in recognizing that there is a subjective element to children acquiring an SEBD label. The quality of support, within the child's environment is central to whether behaviour improves or worsens, whether social problems are recognized and social development supported, and whether emotional development is seen as important as learning development.

Conclusion

In this chapter some of the difficulties children may experience with social, emotional and behavioural development have been discussed and the complex causes for SEBD in young children have been explored with reference to environmental factors. There are no single or simple explanation for most SEBD in children, although there are links with some specific disabilities and deficits in children's early social and emotional experiences.

3

The Framework of Support for Children with Behavioural, Social and Emotional Difficulties

In this chapter the framework for assessment and support of children with behavioural, emotional and social issues will be discussed, with reference to the Special Educational Needs Code of Practice and other relevant policy.

In recent years there have been rapid and unprecedented levels of policy development in the fields of both early years and SEN, including bringing early years settings under the Code of Practice guidelines (DfES 2001). There are a number of different policy initiatives driving the SEN and early years agendas at present, with significant overlap in terms of themes and goals. Key themes across all current early years SEN policy are early identification and intervention, partnership with parents and effective coordinated multi-agency interventions. These features have been embedded in all aspects of the Every Child Matters agenda (DfES 2003) and in one of the standards of the National Service Framework for Children, Young People and Maternity Services (DoH 2004).

This chapter briefly outlines current key policy developments and focuses on the Code of Practice in more detail. However, it is important that readers are aware that the policy agenda is complex and developing, and that as practitioners, students and interested individuals you will need to use the Government Internet sites to keep pace with the changes. There are a number of key advisory documents mentioned in this chapter, for which website addresses and other sources of further information are listed in the reference section at the end of the book.

To summarize, this chapter will help the reader achieve the following learning outcomes:

♦ understand the policy and guidance framework underpinning support for children with behavioural, social and emotional issues

♦ understand the role of settings and practitioners within this

♦ understand the principles of inclusion and partnership central to the policy and guidance

♦ identify key factors in recognizing, referring and assessing children with behavioural, social and emotional issues.

The procedural requirements for working in partnership with parents and other agencies and the roles of practitioners will be discussed here, but there are separate chapters on Working in Partnership and Supporting Children with Behavioural, Social and Emotional Issues in the setting which deal with these areas in much more detail.

Legislation, guidelines and procedures

The Special Educational Needs Code of Practice

The Special Educational Needs Code of Practice (DfES 2001), first introduced in 1994 and updated to the current version in 2001, is the key policy guidance document for the support of children with SEN in early years settings and schools. The Code of Practice is detailed and comprehensive, designed to direct the actions of practitioners in identifying, assessing and supporting children with SEN. However, the Code of Practice also has a major role in determining resource allocation in an area of education where resources are limited and demand is high. As such, definitions of different levels of assessment and intervention and criteria for access to these are complex and difficult for practitioners – nevermind parents – to understand and comply with. The Code is based on a range of principles that support 'good practice' and equity for children with SEN and their families. These principles support the concept of 'rights' for children and parents within this complex system, including the right for parents to receive support and guidance in accessing that system. As such, the principle of partnership with parents is emphasized within the current policy in order to promote equity and to ensure that the parental role is acknowledged and worked with more than in the past.

Further, the complexities of entitlements to resources to support children with SEN have created the need for a partnership service in order for parents to be able to access information and the SEN systems.

The purpose of the Code of Practice is to give practical guidance to schools and early years settings and other involved agencies on policies and procedures with the stated aims of enabling pupils with SEN to:

- ◆ reach their full potential

- ◆ to be included fully in their school communities

- ◆ make a successful transition to adulthood. (DfES 2001: 1: 1)

The requirement to have a Code of Practice is now part of the Education Act 1996, but the Code itself is not part of the law. However, schools, early years settings and all other involved agencies and professionals, such as health and social work, must take the provisions of the Code into account in their work with children with SEN and in decision-making about meeting their needs. In addition, statutory duties introduced in the Special Educational Needs and Disability Act 2001 are part of the Code.

The initial introduction of the Code of Practice focused attention on the needs of children with SEN and tried to redress the neglect of these children's needs that had been apparent in some schools previously. The revised Code enshrines the requirements and duties of the SEN and Disability Act 2001 as mentioned above, and also includes changes to the guidance based on experiences of utilizing the previous version. The changes to statutory duties and requirements in the 2001 Code are:

♦ a stronger right for children with SEN to be educated at a mainstream school

♦ new duties on LAs to arrange for parents of children with SEN to be provided with services offering advice and information and a means of resolving disputes

♦ a new duty on schools and relevant nursery education providers to tell parents when they are making special educational provision for their child

♦ a new right for schools and relevant nursery education providers to request a statutory assessment of a child'. (DfES 2001: iv)

The Code of Practice is based on important principles about working with children with SEN. These principles embody some key ideas about working with children and families, including concepts of partnership and equality. They are:

♦ a child with SEN should have their needs met

♦ the special educational needs of children will normally be met in mainstream schools or settings

♦ the views of the child should be sought and taken into account

♦ parents have a vital role to play in supporting their child's education

♦ children with SEN should be offered full access to a broad, balanced and relevant education, including an appropriate curriculum for the foundation stage and the National Curriculum. (DfES 2001: 1: 5)

The Special Educational Needs and Disability Act 2001 amended the Disability Discrimination Act 1995 to require schools to ensure that children with disabilities are not discriminated against in terms of admissions, exclusions and educational services on the grounds of their disability. Schools are required to ensure disabled children are not treated less fairly than other children because of their disability and that steps are taken to ensure they are not disadvantaged by their disability.

The guiding principle underpinning the Code of Practice is the notion of inclusion, which has replaced the concept of integration. Integration implies placing children with SEN into an existing educational system, with additional support in order for that system to meet the child's needs, whereas inclusion implies that the planning and providing of education is based around the diverse needs of all children. Ideally, inclusion means that the educational system is designed to meet the needs of children with SEN as much as those of other children. However, there are those who argue that the narrowness and prescriptive nature of the early years curricula may militate against genuine inclusion. In addition, the rapid rate of policy development to embed inclusion into settings across the early years may not, in all areas, be supported fully with relevant resources and training. Inclusive policies are also not always fully supported by parents groups, who argue that many children may get better support through special schools, rather than under-resourced mainstream settings.

There is also a strong emphasis on early identification of SEN, as both a principle for providing the best support to children with SEN and ensuring that they receive the services they need at the earliest

possible stage, and a recognition that late identification can be costly.

The Code also places timescales on various aspects
of the SEN processes, including requirements to
review children's educational targets and outcomes at
regular intervals, and timescales for statutory assessments to reduce the very long delays in this process
which have been a feature in the past.

To summarize, the key principles underpinning the
Code of Practice are:

♦ inclusiveness (mainstream schooling for most
  children with SEN, meeting all children's needs)

♦ timeliness (early identification, monitoring and
  review processes)

♦ partnership (with children, parents and other
  agencies)

♦ quality (providing good standards of education to all
  children).

Defining SEN within the Code of Practice

The Code of Practice states that children have SEN
if they have a learning difficulty that requires special
educational provision. A learning difficulty is defined
as being where a child has significantly more difficulty
in learning than other children of a similar age and/or
the child has problems accessing the usual educational facilities available for children because she has
a disability. This definition also includes children under
statutory school age. Special educational provision

refers to different or additional provision than that which is available to most children, or in the case of children under 2 years, any educational provision (DfES 2001:1:3).

However, Skidmore (2004: 15) points out that the definition used in the Code of Practice is somewhat circular and assumes that there is 'a local norm of educational provision' which is insufficient to meet the needs of children with SEN, because they have SEN. There is no recognition within this definition that there may be issues about the extent to which educational provision may be inadequate in meeting the needs of all children.

The role of the Children's Services Authority

This is described in the Code as the role of the LA. This role is primarily aimed at supporting children, parents and settings to ensure the services to children are timely, appropriate and effective. The main functions of the Children's Services Authority (CSA) are:

♦ the needs of children and young people with SEN are identified and assessed quickly and matched by appropriate provision

♦ high-quality support is provided for schools and early education settings, including partnership with educational psychology and other support services, and arrangements for sharing good practice in provision for children and young people with SEN

♦ children and young people with SEN can benefit from coordinated provision by developing close partnerships with parents, schools, health and social services and the voluntary sector

♦ strategic planning for SEN is carried out in consultation with schools and others to develop systems for monitoring and accountability for SEN. (DfES 2001: 1: 11)

In terms of direct interventions with individual children, responsibility for children on the lower levels of the graduated approach lies mainly with settings. However, LAs have responsibility for statemented children, both in terms of procedure and resources. As such, CSAs also have a duty to provide for statutory assessment of children, where this has been agreed. CSAs provide central support services to fulfil their role, including educational psychologists and advisory teachers to assist settings and schools with assessment and planning interventions for individual children. For example, when a setting has identified a child with learning difficulties that have not been improved through differentiated activities, the CSA may then be asked to provide support in the form of an advisory teacher to suggest alternative strategies and to assess the child's needs. An educational psychologist may then be involved in further assessment and to advise on the child's needs, for example, to identify specific disabilities such as dyslexia.

They also provide partnership services to parents, as discussed in further detail below. A key role is to develop local policy, currently focused on educating the majority of children with SEN in mainstream schools.

SEN in the early years

All government grant-funded early years settings and schools are required to have regard for the Code of Practice and to have a SEN policy, which is available to parents and which is regularly reviewed. School governors must ensure that their annual report includes discussion of how SEN policy is being implemented in the school. Settings are also required to have a Special Educational Needs Coordinator (SENCO), now often called an Inclusion Coordinator. Although there are specific roles for Heads of settings and SENCOs/Inclusion Coordinators in supporting children with SEN, there is strong emphasis within the Code on whole-setting involvement in developing and supporting inclusion for children with SEN.

The Role of the SENCO/Inclusion Coordinator

The Early Years SENCO has a key role in implementing SEN policy in the setting. The designated practitioner (sometimes the head or head of setting in smaller institutions) has the role of:

♦ advising and providing support to other practitioners in the setting

♦ liaising with parents and professionals from other agencies

♦ ensuring Individual Education Plans (IEPs) are established, monitored and reviewed for all children with SEN

◆ developing and sharing background information about the child as appropriate

◆ keeping records on all children with statements, Early Years Action or Early Years Action Plus

◆ coordinating the day-to-day delivery of the curriculum and support to children with SEN in line with the individual child's IEP.

In primary schools SENCOs also have a role in developing policy, managing and coordinating the implementation of the SEN policy, managing support staff and contributing to training for staff in the school around SEN issues. SENCOs ideally should have considerable experience and training in SEN and should be familiar with the Code of Practice and other relevant policy. They should have good links with other relevant agencies and skills for working with parents who may be distressed or angry. However, there is some evidence that SENCOs may have difficulties with securing sufficient time for their role, as many have a significant teaching role. There may also be limitations on time and funding for SENCOs to access relevant training and developmental activities.

A key aspect of the role for SENCOs is making decisions about the child's inclusion in and progress through the graduated levels of SEN support. This role includes consideration of the following factors:

◆ assessment outcomes, e.g. test scores, educational psychologist evaluations

- the child's levels of attainment

- the views of relevant teaching and support staff

- parent's views

- the level of success with previous and current interventions.

Dyson and Millward (2000) argue that SENCOs need the following skills in order to perform this role:

- analysing and interpreting evidence relating to students' levels of performance and difficulties

- understanding the resources available for special needs provision in the school and LA and matching both the available resources and the possible forms of provision to levels and patterns of student need

- understanding the procedures of and criteria used by the LA and a range of external services and relating these to particular cases

- negotiating with class teachers, LA service members, LA officers and parents to secure appropriate provision for students.

Dyson and Millward (2000) also argue that SENCOs make decisions about children within a political context, not just on the basis of independent criteria. This context includes the views of parents, and of colleagues from within the school and the LA, and the SENCO's knowledge about resource constraints. To this extent, decision-making may be more intuitive, based on the range of views and evidence the SENCO has access to, rather than criteria-led.

SENCOs working with children with SEBD may face particular difficulties in balancing the range of views on the best plan for a child. As practitioners struggle to cope with behavioural problems in the setting and press for additional resources, parents may have different views about what works best for their child.

Harriet, 6 years old

By the age of 6 it was becoming evident that Harriet had some social and emotional difficulties, which were probably associated with ASD. However, at that point Harriet's behaviour in class was not a cause for concern and she was keeping up with other children in learning activities. Harriet's parents were reluctant to start the statementing process because they felt it 'labelled' their child. The school was able to support Harriet's social needs, to some extent, within the existing resource base, and Harriet was also receiving support from health services. The SENCO also felt that Harriet's needs would grow as time went on and her learning difficulties become more apparent. She suggested that they should consider statementing at a later stage when there was more concrete evidence of learning difficulties, but before Harriet went to secondary school, in order to secure resources for the future.

Area Early Years SENCOs

Area Early Years SENCOS were established to offer non-maintained settings that deliver Foundation Stage provision the support they need for inclusion. Area SENCOs support about 20 settings each, offering advice and helping settings make links with other agencies such as health and social care. The role was established to ensure that non-maintained settings outside the local authority context get the help they need to follow the Code of Practice and to develop inclusive approaches to supporting children with SEN and their families.

Individual Education Plans (IEPs) and Reviews

IEPs are required for all children who are identified as having SEN. They include:

♦ a record of the child's learning difficulties

♦ targets for development

♦ details of how the child's development will be supported

♦ parental views and contributions

♦ monitoring and review arrangements.

IEPs are reviewed at least twice a year, preferably three times. Reviews are arranged by the SENCO, and parents and other involved professionals are invited. The child's progress towards meeting developmental targets is discussed and new targets agreed. In addition, any new or ongoing concerns are shared and plans made to provide new and/or different types of support where necessary. Parental involvement is very important and this will be discussed further in Chapter 5: Working in Partnership.

The involvement of other professionals, where applicable, is also crucial to ensuring the child receives the range of services she needs and that these are effectively coordinated to benefit the child and family.

Dan, 7 years old

Dan has just been to a full multi-disciplinary paediatric assessment organized by the health service at the request of his parents. The assessment confirmed the Educational Psychologist's report that Dan has a specific learning disability (severe dyslexia) but no general learning difficulties. However, the assessment also determined that Dan is dyspraxic to some extent, and that physiotherapy is recommended to support the development of his coordination, balance and concentration. The SENCO invites the physiotherapist to Dan's review and she agrees to 'train' two of the teaching assistants, who have regular involvement with Dan, to do the exercises with him at school. Dan's parents are pleased and relieved that he is not going to miss school, and they are not going to miss work, to travel five miles to the hospital, three times a week, for the physiotherapy.

Reviews are key occasions for those involved with the child to share views and opinions, new information and ideas about effective support strategies. SENCOs have a responsibility to try and ensure reviews are scheduled at times that parents and others can attend and that parents are supported to engage with the review and make their own contributions. However, the time and resource limitations discussed above may possibly reduce the responsiveness of SENCOs to parents' and other professionals' timescales in some situations.

Early years/Foundation Stage settings

Early years settings have become increasingly significant in the process of identifying and supporting children with SEN as early identification and intervention is more likely to ensure the child has a better outcome and is also cost-effective. Early years settings are required to ensure they have policies and practices in place to ensure children with SEN are identified where possible. However, there are considerable differences in the developmental patterns of children with SEN depending on the type of SEN and any underlying disability. For some children, identification of SEBD may be difficult in a pre-school setting because it is unclear whether the difficulties the child is experiencing are short term or longer term. Developmental delays of a less severe nature may not immediately be identified as such, as they may be considered to be a natural variation in developmental stage common to children in the early years.

The Code emphasizes a graduated approach to identifying, assessing and responding to children with SEN, within a whole-setting approach. There is considerable flexibility in how this approach can be organized within different settings to take into account the wide range of different types of early years provision. This approach will include:

♦ monitoring all children's progress and attainment

♦ identifying children who have ongoing difficulties which are not resolved by normal differentiation of activities

♦ Early Years Action

♦ Early Years Action Plus

♦ statutory assessment.

Key factors in judging whether a child has SEN are whether 'additional' or 'different' actions in terms of the child's learning result in him making adequate progress. This is to ensure that children who may be starting from a different baseline of developmental progress are not deemed to have SEN because they have peers at a more advanced stage of development. If a child responds to differentiation of the curriculum by, for example, making more progress than previously or not falling further behind, then the child would not necessarily be seen as having SEN, although good practice would include continued monitoring of the child's progress.

Early Years Action and Action Plus

Early Years Action refers to different or additional support for children, where SEN have been identified by either the practitioners or parents. Good practice would ensure that parents are involved in any decision to make differential educational provision for the child, and that relevant background information would be gathered from the parents and any other involved professionals. The point at which the decision to take action is determined is a matter of judgment and the SENCO advises and supports practitioners seeking advice about a specific child. An educational psychologist may also assess the child, and advice may be sought and given from an advisory teacher from the LA. The Code of Practice gives the following advice about when Early Years Action should be considered:

> The triggers for intervention through Early Years Action could be the practitioners' or parents' concern about a child who despite receiving appropriate early education experiences:
>
> ◆ makes little or no progress even when teaching approaches are particularly targeted to improve the child's identified area of weakness;
>
> ◆ continues working at levels significantly below those expected for children of a similar age in certain areas;
>
> ◆ presents persistent emotional and/or behavioural difficulties, which are not ameliorated by the behaviour management techniques usually employed in the setting;
>
> ◆ has sensory or physical problems, and continues to make little or no progress despite the provision of personal aids and equipment;

◆ has communication and/or interaction difficulties, and requires specific individual interventions in order to access learning. (DfEs 2001: 4: 21)

Early Years Action Plus is the stage of intervention when children receiving additional support as described above also have the involvement of professionals from other agencies in assessing, planning, target-setting and providing educational strategies or resources to support the child's learning and development. Early Years Action Plus may result from the child failing to make expected progress despite Early Years Action.

The triggers for referral for seeking help from outside agencies could be that, despite receiving an individualized programme and/or concentrated support, the child:

◆ continues to make little or no progress in specific areas over a long period;

◆ continues working at an early years curriculum substantially below that expected of children of a similar age;

◆ has emotional or behavioural difficulties which substantially and regularly interfere with the child's own learning or that of the group, despite having an individualized behaviour management programme;

◆ has sensory or physical needs, and requires additional equipment or regular visits for direct intervention or advice by practitioners from a specialist service;

◆ has ongoing communication or interaction difficulties that impede the development of social relationships and cause substantial barriers to learning. (DfES 2001: 4: 31)

Chris, 3 and a half years old

Chris was an adopted child who joined his new family at the age of 2 and a half years. Chris had experienced severe neglect and several changes of carers in his very early years. In nursery, Chris was uncooperative and angry, often refusing to do as he was asked and lashing out at other children. He did not join in play and was unable to relate to other children. Chris often appeared under stress, upset or withdrawn in nursery. Although clearly very bright, Chris was not making progress in his play or learning.

Early Years Action
With his parents' agreement, Chris spent some of the day separate from the other children, playing with a single practitioner. He did some planned activities with the practitioner when he could be persuaded to and he had a space for 'time out' from the group when he became upset. The object was to help Chris build a relationship with one practitioner through which he could access play and learning and enjoy the setting.

Early Years Action Plus
At age 4, Chris' behaviour was not improving and he was still finding it very difficult to be in the group without becoming angry and aggressive or withdrawing. Chris was trying to access 'time out' space for most of the day

and his learning was not progressing, despite occasional glimpses of considerable ability. Chris was becoming more likely to refuse to do as he was asked and he retreated into a very distressed state if anyone persisted with instructions. At this point, Chris' parents and the setting agreed to contact Child and Adolescent Mental Health Services (CAMHS) where Chris was referred for assessment and support. Chris started play therapy at CAMHS to support his emotional development and to start to identify and resolve some of his attachment issues. The therapist attended Chris' reviews and advised both parents and the setting on how to help him with learning and development.

Statutory assessments and statement of SEN

For some children, even multi-agency intervention does not ensure progress. At this stage, the setting and/or the parents (or possibly another professional concerned with the child's development, such as a health visitor or GP) may suggest statutory assessment for SEN. This process is available for children aged 2 years and over. Statutory assessment is a multi-disciplinary assessment to determine whether a statement of SEN should be made in respect of the child. However, not all children receive statutory assessments when these are requested. In order for the assessment to be agreed by the LA, the child's needs must be severe and complex and the provision available through Early Years Action and Action Plus must be shown to be insufficient to effectively support the child. The issues the child faces must be long-term and affect educational progress significantly. Some of the case studies in this book demonstrate some of the issues that may lead to statementing, for example, Harriet was statemented for social and behavioural issues linked to ASD, and Chris was also statemented because his attachment issues and early neglect led to long-term SEBD.

Not all children with SEN are assessed or statemented for SEN. The statutory assessment process is a way of both identifying children who will get long-term additional resources, and a way of gate-keeping access to those resources.

The statement outlines the child's SEN and the views of parents and key professionals on the child's needs. It also outlines the services being made available and the contributions of involved agencies. Finally, the statement includes monitoring and review arrangements.

Primary school-aged children with SEN

Children entering primary school may or may not have already been identified as having a SEN. If there is already an IEP in place, the child's information and plans will be transferred to school. Other children's SEN may not be identified until primary school, either because the learning difficulty was not apparent in the early years setting or because the child did not attend a pre-school.

Information about the child may come from a variety of sources including parents, the Foundation Stage profile from the child's early years setting, and observations of the child's performance and behaviour on starting school. If there are concerns about the child, a similar graduated approach is followed as in the Foundation Stage, including School Action and Action Plus.

The triggers for intervention through School Action could be the teachers' or others' concern, underpinned by evidence, about a child who despite receiving differentiated learning opportunities:

♦ makes little or no progress even when teaching approaches are targeted, particularly in a child's identified area of weakness;

♦ shows signs of difficulty in developing literacy or mathematics skills which result in poor attainment in some curriculum areas;

♦ presents persistent emotional or behavioural difficulties which are not ameliorated by the behaviour management techniques usually employed in the school;

♦ has sensory or physical problems, and continues to make little or no progress despite the provision of specialist equipment;

♦ has communication and/or interaction difficulties, and continues to make little or no progress despite the provision of a differentiated curriculum. (DfES 2001: 5: 44)

School Action Plus would be considered if, despite the measures taken at School Action level, the child continues to make little progress, remains below the National Curriculum levels expected for children of the same age and continues to have problems with literacy and mathematics skills development. Children with EBD which 'substantially and regularly interferes with the child's own learning or that of the class group' despite steps taken at School Action level and an individual behaviour plan, would be considered for School Action Plus. Involving other professionals and agencies requires the agreement and involvement of parents and a clear idea of the type of support the child would need. Therefore, School Action Plus may involve other professionals with specific expertise who may advise the setting or school staff; be involved with further assessment of the child; or work directly with the child.

Statutory assessment in primary schools takes place in a similar way to early years statutory assessment. However, there will be a wider range of factors to take into account with an older child, including the range of interventions and support already accessed, the outcomes of reviews over a longer period of time and the child's progress within the National Curriculum. For some children with specific or identifiable disabilities or sensory impairments, early identification may be reasonably straightforward. For other children, the process of identifying learning difficulties may take place in school rather than early years settings because it has been important to build a picture of the child's developmental pattern over time to establish that a learning difficulty exists and is long-term and seriously affecting the child's ability to learn. This longer process may be more likely for some children with SEBD, as the extent and nature of their difficulties may only emerge over time.

Harriet, 4 years old

At 4 years some of Harriet's social and emotional issues were apparent. She had difficulty judging other children's social cues and responding to them so she found it difficult to join play. Harriet liked to be with other children but often failed to follow their conversation or make appropriate responses. She was acutely sensitive to noise and would become stressed and angry if other children were noisy or boisterous near her. However, it was unclear to both her parents and the practitioners as to whether this was a significant problem or a shorter-term developmental delay.

Other children who may have a specific disability that affects behavioural, social and emotional development such as autism or ADHD may be identified earlier. Key factors are the persistence of the difficulties, their impact on the child's learning and the lack of improvement within the setting, despite interventions to support the child.

The Code of Practice provides a comprehensive framework for early identification and intervention. However, it has been criticized for maintaining a complex and bureaucratic system, which may be hard to access for parents, children and practitioners. There are also many issues about whether resources are sufficient to support the intentions of the Code, especially in relation to:

♦ developing inclusive practices

♦ support for children and parents within settings

♦ support and advice for settings, practitioners and SENCOs from the CSA

♦ SENCO time and training

♦ developing effective communication networks

♦ developing effective multi-disciplinary working.

Parent partnership

One of the key principles of the Code of Practice is ensuring that parents are fully involved in the decision-making and planning processes around their children's learning and support needs. This principle is in line with general policy developments in early years and primary education to ensure that parents have a clearer and better informed 'voice' in their children's educational arrangements. However, there is also an acknowledgement that parents of children with SEN may have a particular need for support because of the stresses of dealing with what can be a complex, bureaucratic SEN system. In addition, some parents with children with SEN may lack the personal and social resources to negotiate these systems and effectively have 'their say'. The terminology and jargon associated with SEN may be incomprehensible to those who do not use it regularly and it may be difficult for some parents to engage with professionals from a range of services, particularly where they have had poor experiences of such professionals previously. For many parents, the sheer overwhelming difficulties of supporting their child's educational needs; understanding what they can do to help; and accessing the best support may be too much on top of the day-to-day stresses of parenting a child with SEBD or other SEN.

Key aspects of parent partnership services are that parents should have access to:

♦ information about processes and services

♦ advice about their children's issues and needs

♦ guidance at key decision-making points.

All CSAs are required to provide parent-partnership services to ensure parents' needs are met during their child's assessment, identification and support planning. The service also supports parents through the process of statementing if this is required, and may provide training on aspects of the procedures.

CSAs also provide independent supporters for parents. An independent parental supporter may:

♦ listen to worries and concerns

♦ provide ongoing and general support

♦ help parents to understand what is happening during SEN procedures and processes such as school action, assessment and statementing

♦ explain rights and responsibilities

♦ help parents to prepare for and attend visits and meetings

♦ help parents to make phone calls, fill in forms and write letters and reports

♦ help parents to express your views and communicate with schools and local authorities

♦ find further sources of information, support and advice. (from Directgov 2006)

CSAs also provide disagreement resolution services to resolve disputes between parents and settings, or CSAs, about any aspect of the child's SEN assessment and provision. These services can be used where informal efforts to come to an agreement about assessment or provision are unsuccessful.

A DfES-commissioned evaluation of parent-partnership services found that in general they were:

♦ valued by parents

♦ enhanced SEN services

♦ based on a commitment to the principle of parent partnership

♦ meeting minimum standards for parent partnership services stated in the Code of Practice.

However, the evaluation also found wide variations in practice across different CSAs in relation to staffing, workloads and budgets, and concluded that smaller CSAs, in particular, may need more support to develop their parent partnership services (Rogers *et al.* 2006).

Children's participation

The Code of Practice supports the principle of children's participation in decision-making about their needs and how to meet them. However, participation is described in terms of the child's ability to give a view or opinion, and how this process can be supported, offering a 'sliding scale' of participation depending on the extent to which communication with the child could be achieved. Clearly, participation is not just about the child's ability to communicate but also about the ethos and practices in the setting, which may support or inhibit that communication.

In a study based in schools, Norwich and Kelly (2006) found that in order for children to participate the school ethos needed to be based on inclusive assumptions which supported all children's rights to participation and valued their views. Other relevant issues are time and space to make relationships with children and to elicit their views, developing a child-centred ethos and guidelines on how to access children's views. Norwich and Kelly (2006) found both formal and informal approaches are used to help children to give their views. Formal processes tended to be around IEP reviews and are more likely to involve SENCOs. Informal processes are more likely to involve teaching assistants who were seen as having more time than teachers to engage with children. Approaches included talking, drawing, recording conversations, and using prompts such as picture cards. However, the difficulties of eliciting the views of very young children and those with cognitive developmental delays and/or communication difficulties were noted. Recently, there has been an increased focus on 'listening to children' in early years settings and it is clear that developing strategies to support children's participation in their own SEN planning and support needs to be in the wider context of improving consultation with, and feedback from, all children.

Chris, 5 years old

In the week before his IEP review, Chris did some reading with a teaching assistant in FS2 on his own. The teaching assistant was someone he knew well and liked. During their time together she asked Chris what he liked about school and what he would like to change. She explained that she wanted to make sure that everyone in the review knew what he felt as he was the most important person involved. She wrote down the things Chris told her and asked him if he would like to say anything in the review. Chris said he didn't want to go to the review but he wanted them to know that he didn't like playtime as the other children ignored him. The teaching assistant wrote this down also and represented Chris' views in the meeting.

Children in need

Although the Code of Practice is the most immediately relevant set of guidelines for those working with children with SEN, it is also important to be aware that some children who have SEN may also be defined as 'children in need' within the Children Act 1989. However, despite a notable overlap, not all 'children in need' have SEN. The term 'child in need' is used to define any child who is considered to require services in order to support a 'reasonable standard' of health and development. This definition covers all children with disabilities and any child who would have 'significantly impaired' health and development if services were not provided.

The Children Act 1989 promotes a multi-disciplinary approach to service provision for 'children in need'. This means that for some children, professionals such as social workers, health visitors and possibly voluntary sector practitioners may already be involved. It is important that arrangements for joint planning and assessment and information sharing between professionals involved are considered at an early stage to ensure children and families have a clear idea of who is offering them what type of support and how services will be delivered. As such, the child's SEN support may be part of the services on offer and there needs to be clear links between this and other aspects of service delivery.

Removing Barriers to Achievement: The Government's strategy for SEN

This strategy is a programme for change, which states how the principles and outcomes outlined in Every Child Matters will be put into practice for children with SEN. The Every Child Matters agenda has five key outcomes:

- be healthy
- stay safe
- enjoy and achieve
- make a positive contribution
- achieve economic well-being.

These outcomes are to be achieved through policy and practice development to bring about more coherent, integrated services for all children. Key changes are:

- the development of multi-agency service delivery
- extended school provision
- information-sharing between professionals
- developing the Common Assessment framework.

The Removing Barriers to Achievement (DfES 2004) strategy builds on previous policy statements supporting early intervention, mainstream provision for most children with SEN and timely, integrated service delivery to children and families. However, it also recognizes that the report Special Educational Needs: A mainstream issue (Audit Commission 2002) found that there were still unacceptable delays in meeting children's needs, children being refused places in mainstream schools, and practitioners unable to meet the diversity of needs within their setting.

The strategy focuses on four key areas for change:

Behavioural, Emotional and Social Difficulties

Early intervention

♦ Improving support for children with special needs from birth.

♦ Improving childcare for children with SEN and disabilities.

♦ Improving SEN advice and support to early years settings.

♦ Raising the skills and awareness of staff in early years settings.

♦ Funding to support early intervention and inclusive practice.

♦ Tackling bureaucracy.

Removing barriers to learning

♦ Widening opportunities in mainstream education.

♦ Transforming special schools.

♦ Developing local communities of schools for local children.

♦ Improving specialist advice and support for schools.

Raising expectations and achievement

♦ Personalizing learning for children with SEN.

♦ Making better use of information on how well children with SEN are progressing in school.

- Developing a flexible curriculum and recognized qualifications for all.

- Involving children and young people with SEN in decision-making.

- Improving opportunities for progression beyond school for young people with learning difficulties and disabilities.

Delivering improvements in partnership

- Monitoring progress and supporting improvements in local authorities.

- Monitoring progress and supporting improvements in schools.

- Building parents' confidence in mainstream education.

- Improving the availability of health and social services and organizing services around the needs of children and their families. (Teachernet 2006)

The strategy draws on the Early Support Pilot to determine that key factors in achieving these aims are:

- more integration of services

- delegated resources

- better support for early years setting from LAs

- focus on the inclusion agenda.

Behavioural, Emotional and Social Difficulties

The key principles of the strategy are:

♦ early identification

♦ integrated service development

♦ raising standards

♦ parent and child participation

♦ delegated funding

♦ mainstream schooling for the majority.

In many ways, this agenda reaffirms and empha-sizes key features of previous policy and restates the principles on which this policy was built. However, the Every Child Matters agenda places improvements for children with SEN in the context of better outcomes for all children and a greater emphasis on integrated service delivery. The challenge that this agenda raises is how to achieve these developments within the existing and potential resource base.

Other Government initiatives to support social and emotional development

Relatively recently, there has been more emphasis on recognizing and responding to children's social and emotional needs as a key factor in successful learning. Although the links between learning and other aspects of development have long been under-stood, strategies to meet children's needs more holistically have been limited in schools particularly, until relatively recently. In early years settings, the Birth to Three Matters framework anc the Foundation Stage curriculum have been more cognisant of the need to support all aspects of children's development. The Birth to Three Matters framework includes 'a strong child', referring to development of a sense of self, belongingness and self-assurance, and also 'a skilful communicator', referring to the development of social and communication skills. The Foundation Stage curriculum includes personal, social and emotional development as one of the early learning goals. However, there have been a number of initiatives in primary schools to support the development of all children's social and emotional aspects of learning. Target areas for development are:

♦ self-awareness

♦ managing feelings

♦ motivation

♦ empathy and social skills.

From May 2005, curriculum resource materials for primary schools have become available to support the development of social and emotional aspects of learning (SEAL), based around seven themes:

♦ new beginnings

♦ getting on and falling out

♦ bullying

♦ going for goals!

Behavioural, Emotional and Social Difficulties

- good to be me
- relationships
- changes.

The resources are different for the range of age groups and are introduced throughout the curriculum on a whole-school basis, although the themes are the same each year.

Behaviour Improvement Programmes (BIPs) have also been implemented in a number of LAs in the UK. These have included strategies such as:

- multi-agency support for pupils at risk of EBD
- learning mentors
- 'extended schools'
- multi-disciplinary approaches to supporting individual children.

These programmes have supported the more general move towards supporting children with SEBD through whole-setting approaches and multi-disciplinary interventions.

The Early Support Programme (www.earlysupport. gov.uk) is the Government's initiative aimed at disabled children under 3 years for 'achieving better coordinated, family-focused services for young disabled children and their families across England'. It is embedded within the broader Every Child Matters programme for developing services to children and families to improve outcomes. Key aspects are integrated service development and delivery, and partnership with parents. The programme shares aims with the National Service Framework for Children, Young People and Maternity Services Core Standard 8, which states:

> Children and young people who are disabled or have complex health needs receive coordinated, high quality child and family-centred services which are based on assessed needs, which promote social inclusion and, where possible, enable them and their families to live ordinary lives.

The programme implements the guidelines for working with young disabled children Together from the Start: Practical guidance for professionals working with disabled children (birth to third birthday) and their families (DoH 2003).

The programme has introduced support materials for both practitioners and families. Key principles are:

♦ better coordination of service delivery and improved continuity of care

♦ joint review and planning

♦ better information for families

♦ multi-agency planning for service development

♦ tracking progress, promoting development and supporting partnership working with families. (www.earlysupport.gov.uk)

Conclusion

In this chapter, some of the key legislation, policy and guidelines underpinning the development of services for children with SEN have been discussed, with emphasis on the SEN Code of Practice as the most significant of these. However, the coverage in this chapter is not exhaustive as the relatively recent Government focus on the early years and children's policy fields has led to an unprecedented level of policy development in these areas.

In the rapidly changing field of early years policy it is important for practitioners to be aware that new policy developments, guidelines and legislation that may influence the care and education of young children with SEN may continue to emerge beyond the publication of any book. In order to keep in touch with new developments and gain a good understanding of policy and practice in the field, practitioners need to regularly access key Government websites. Suggested sites are:

♦ DfES – www.dfes.gov.uk

♦ Early Support – www.earlysupport.gov.uk

♦ Every Child Matters – www.everychildmatters.gov. uk

♦ Sure Start – www.surestart.gov.uk

♦ Teachernet – www.teachernet.gov.uk

4

Supporting Children with Behavioural, Emotional and Social Difficulties in the Setting

In this chapter we look at the ways in which children with SEBD can be supported in the setting; within the frameworks and policy outlined in Chapter 3; and with reference to both whole-setting development and individual practitioner responses. The role of settings in early identification and intervention will be explored. The development of inclusion policies and strategies for supporting the social and learning development of children with behavioural, emotional and social issues will also be discussed.

This chapter will help the reader:

♦ understand whole-setting development to support children with behavioural, emotional and social SEN

♦ understand the individual practitioner's role in supporting children with behavioural, emotional and social SEN

♦ develop effective inclusive policies and strategies for supporting social and learning development

♦ develop strategies for managing behaviour to support development.

What are the best approaches to supporting children with SEBD?

Skidmore suggests that the approach taken to support the education of children with learning difficulties has traditionally depended on the view of why learning difficulties arise (2004: 10). Skidmore goes on to suggest that there are two differing forms of pedagogical discourse on the education of children with learning difficulties (2004: 113). Firstly, the discourse of deviance, which supports the view that educational failure is due to factors inherent in the child and that the setting's response should focus on the child's deficits, including providing a differentiated version of the curriculum for that child. The discourse of inclusion, on the other hand, suggests that educational failure is due to 'insufficiently responsive presentation of the curriculum' and that the setting should focus on developing the curriculum and pedagogy to help teachers learn how to effectively engage all children in learning.

Skidmore's discussion is helpful in reminding us that inclusion is about ensuring that the pedagogies and curricula are developed with a view to meeting the needs of all children. This concept of a broad-based curriculum is important when considering the sorts of support that might best help children with SEBD. It is important to remember that children's behaviour is contextual and that changes to the learning environment and learning activities can be central to any successful strategy to support children with SEBD.

Jake, 6 years old

Jake is sitting in class watching the other children as they do individual, quiet reading. He has a book in front of him but he cannot read a word and he has no helper at this time of day. The teacher is listening to other children read to him one-by-one. Jake is not going to get any help with the book and he is uncomfortable, angry and bored. The teacher gets up and quietly calls Jake to the computer. He helps him access a programme he has worked on before and makes sure he has started the sequence successfully. The teacher goes back to listening to the other children read.

How effective would this strategy be in supporting Jake's emotional development and learning? Consider other approaches to this situation and discuss with a colleague or mentor.

The best approaches, then, to supporting the learning and development of children with SEN are those that encompass all aspects of the learning environment, learning activities and relationships, and routines and systems within the setting. All these factors can be referred to as a whole-setting approach.

Whole-settings approaches to inclusion of children with SEBD

Whole-setting approaches encompass the policies, practices, ethos and goals, management structures and leadership, communications systems and relationships of a setting in relation to a particular area of work. This type of approach also includes the behaviour and attitudes of practitioners and the ways in which the setting promotes its values and practices to others. In order for individual practitioners to be able to effectively promote inclusion for all children, they need to be working within the context of a whole-setting approach. Whole-setting approaches to inclusion mean that all aspects of the setting are focused on inclusive policies and practices. Weare argues that 'analyses and solutions that work in practice are usually holistic ones' when discussing emotionally literate schools, and this view applies to other aspects of whole-setting development towards inclusive practice (2004: 53).

Effective whole-setting approaches to inclusion mean:

♦ shared, clear goals and understandings of what is expected

♦ practitioners are supported in a collaborative environment

♦ policy is co-constructed with practitioners, parents and children

♦ relevant training is available to practitioners

♦ inclusive practices are evaluated and developed

♦ emotional literacy is a key element of policy and practice.

Whole-setting approaches are developed through ensuring that inclusion is central to every agenda within the setting and that inclusive practice is at the heart of decision-making and policy development within the setting. Clearly, leadership styles and management commitment to inclusion are central to developing whole-setting approaches. In order to develop whole-setting approaches to supporting children with SEBD, managers need to:

♦ be clear in their understanding of the needs of the children in their care who are experiencing SEBD

♦ have effective systems for communicating with practitioners, parents and other professionals about children with SEBD

♦ have a well-defined and publicized strategy for supporting all children's emotional, social and behavioural development within the setting

♦ have skills and knowledge about how to work with other agencies and professionals to support children with SEBD

♦ have created environments that support all aspects of children's development and which minimize behavioural issues arising

♦ provide support for all practitioners to develop their understandings of inclusion and their practice in this area.

The role of the individual practitioner is, to a great extent, determined by the whole-setting approach, as discussed above. As with many aspects of practitioner development, it is difficult for practitioners to achieve good standards of practice in a setting where policies and practice are poorly considered and resourced, or where there is lack of clarity about the expectations or underpinning principles guiding staff behaviour in the setting.

Supporting children with SEBD is an area where there are many variations in standards of practice and access to staff development opportunities for individuals. According to a study by Berger (ICAN Conference 2006), training for staff in supporting children's mental health (emotional and behavioural development) is currently inadequate. Berger argues that the focus in schools, for example, is on managing problem behaviour, not promoting children's well-being. In addition, partnerships are not always effective, as they need to be inclusive in all aspects of school.

Supporting children's social and emotional development

Children's social and emotional development are discussed in Chapter 1 and some of the difficulties that may arise in these areas of development, and possible contributory factors, are discussed in Chapter 2. However, it is worth reiterating at this point that there are very clear links between children's difficulties with social and emotional aspects of development and both learning difficulties and behavioural problems. Not only are these aspects linked but they may create a self-reinforcing system within which the child's social, emotional, behavioural and cognitive developmental difficulties reinforce each other, and are possibly reinforced by the child's environments, to result in a negative spiral of escalating behavioural problems, consolidated learning difficulties and increasing emotional distress. The case example of Dan in Chapter 2 highlights how this negative system can develop for young children and how this can system can be reinforced by the child's lowered self-esteem and diminishing self-confidence.

Increasingly, we understand that creating environments that support all children's social and emotional development are central to ensuring that fewer children develop difficulties in this area. However, it is important to remember that children's main influences are probably outside the setting and practitioners alone may not achieve sufficient change. Partnership with parents is discussed in Chapter 5.

In this section, some aspects of supporting children's social and emotional development will be discussed, with reference to developing these with a whole-setting approach.

Forming relationships with children

During recent training events around attachment in settings in which the author was involved, it became clear through the discussion which took place that some practitioners were hesitant to make warm and mutually satisfying relationships with children because they were concerned both about child abuse allegations and children transferring attachments from parents to themselves. As such, some practitioners were sometimes actively avoiding touching children or showing affection or special concern for them.

However, children make a range of attachments and develop new attachments throughout their childhoods and positive experiences of attachment will create a pre-disposition for good relationships in the future. Avoiding emotional and physical contact with children is not child protecting, but may be an attempt to protect adults against the unlikely event of a child abuse allegation, while denying the child the right to warmth and affection.

There are a reasons why these concerns may arise:

♦ Child protection issues may not be discussed sufficiently in settings, and procedures may be over-concerned with adult protection.

♦ The nature and value of multiple attachments for children and the importance of developing warm, secure relationships through which children can grow and learn is not always sufficiently understood.

♦ Key worker systems are sometimes seen as administrative rather than as the focus for the development of special relationships.

The following case examples illustrate the difference in experiences some children may have.

Suzy, 5 years old

A PGCE student related how Suzy had fallen in the playground and had cut her knee quite badly. The student, who was male, asked her to follow him and, weeping, she walked to the medical room behind him, knee bleeding as she walked. In the room, he asked Suzy to sit on a chair, but left the door open and then went to find a female teaching assistant. Suzy continued to weep. The teaching assistant gave Suzy swabs and she cleaned up her knee and then she gave her a plaster to put on her knee. The student felt the whole event was successful as the child had not been touched during the incident. Suzy continued to weep. The student had been told to avoid touching the children at all while on placement to avoid child protection issues arising.

Ginny, 3 years old

Ginny was the youngest at nursery, attending just after her third birthday to support her slow development and limited social skills. Ginny loved nursery but got very tired as the session came to close. When her mother collected her she usually found her sitting on her key worker's knee having a story or a sing song with other children, happy and comfortable, eyes drooping and ready for a nap. The key worker checked with Ginny's mother that this was OK and always gave Ginny a hug before handing over to her mother. Ginny's mother saw

> the practitioner's warmth for her child with great relief and felt it validated her decision to send Ginny to nursery.

The first case illustrates a dilemma for settings in ensuring adults are protected from false allegations of abuse, while children have their emotional needs supported. There are no easy answers to these types of dilemmas but children's needs have to be considered in any policy-making in this area.

In order to promote effective relationships between children and practitioners settings should:

◆ have a key worker system with a clear understanding that developing good relationships with the child and parents is the basis of this role

◆ establish regular monitoring of children through observation and assessment, and effective planning and recording systems

◆ have a child-centred child protection policy

◆ develop policies and an ethos which promote warm, respectful relationships between all children and all adults

◆ provide training and staff development to support a good understanding of the role of attachments in children's development

◆ create an environment and activities that all children can learn and develop in and from, without barriers or increased difficulties for some

- create an environment which acknowledges cultural and lifestyle differences and different cultural norms and behaviour.

Practitioners should:

- actively develop warm and affectionate relation-ships with all children in their care
- value and respect all children and parents
- listen to children and share ideas thoughts, memories and events with them
- use observation to inform themselves about children's interests, abilities, social situation, states of mind and emotional states
- keep appropriate records and share these with managers and colleagues
- be sensitive to events in the child's life and available for the child to share events, ideas thoughts and feelings
- give detailed and considered praise to the child and comment positively on progress
- encourage the child to make their own decisions and act independently
- provide opportunities for success and achievement for every child.

Early identification

Early identification simply means that practitioners should be aware that children with SEBD can be supported much more effectively if their difficulties are identified at an early stage and responded to appropriately. However, in practice early identification can be difficult. Children may go through periods of emotional disruption leading to social shyness, withdrawal or isolation, or become disruptive and/or aggressive for a wide variety of reasons such as:

- ◆ joining a setting/group for the first time

- ◆ struggling with learning because of limited previous experience, age, stage of development, EAL, cultural difference to the setting

- ◆ lack of previous social experiences

- ◆ different language background to other children and practitioners

- ◆ changes within the home, e.g. birth of a new child, separation of parents or joining a new step-family, illness

- ◆ lack of effective approaches to making and supporting relationships in the setting.

With appropriate assessment, planning and support for the child in conjunction with parents, and the development and application of relevant policies in the setting, most children's social, emotional and behavioural difficulties can be transitory. If issues are quickly identified and responded to sensitively, most children going through these experiences can be helped to become more emotionally stable and more socially capable. Inappropriate intervention, on the other hand, may lead to more difficulties if a child's self-esteem is damaged. For example, it is important to recognize that not all children with EAL have learning difficulties.

The problem may be in identifying when some children have more deep-rooted difficulties that may require a more lengthy and detailed strategy of intervention. Children who may have more extensive SEBD may include:

◆ those with learning difficulties

◆ those who have suffered abuse and/or neglect

◆ 'looked after' children

◆ those who experience lack of warmth in the family home, and/or a chaotic lifestyle, drugs or alcohol or domestic violence

◆ those who have a disability which may lead to learning difficulties such as ASD or ADHD, and have been identified as having social and behavioural issues that are part of the disability

◆ asylum-seeking children or newly immigrated children where there have been major disruptive life events and transitions, including loss of home and family members

◆ children who have been socially isolated for whatever reason.

In all these cases, and others, SEBD may be a possibility and it is important to plan and deliver support at the earliest possible stage to ensure that the child receives the best response.

Behavioural, Emotional and Social Difficulties

Settings can promote early identification of SEBD by:

◆ ensuring all children's learning, social and behavioural progress is observed, monitored and appropriate records are kept

◆ sharing information and consulting with parents about any concerns and background information

◆ encouraging parents to seek support/assessment from other agencies such as health services if there is the possibility of an unidentified disability

◆ ensuring that practitioners share concerns with each other and with their managers

◆ sharing information with other agencies and professionals with parental permission

◆ involving local authority SEN support services for advice and assessment at an early stage

◆ listening to the child's preoccupations and concerns and building relationships with the child.

The key to effective early identification is well-trained staff who have the skills to recognize the difference between short-term and longer-term difficulties, and policies and management support for this process.

Key questions to ask when determining if a child's SEBD requires further action could include:

◆ Has the child just gone through a difficult experience or transition?

◆ Have the child's emotional, social and behavioural issues responded to support within the setting?

◆ Have the difficulties been the result of more serious issues as listed above?

◆ Has the child's learning development responded to differentiation or extra support or have learning difficulties persisted?

◆ Have the child's behavioural problems disrupted her learning?

◆ Are there concerns from parents or other professionals about the child?

◆ Has the SENCO been involved and what are her views?

Once practitioners are sure that there are SEBD, then the SENCO will need to be more involved and the child might be placed on Early years Action or Action Plus as discussed in Chapter 3.

Early support for social and emotional difficulties

A key aspect of support is making relationships with each child in the setting, as discussed above, to ensure that every child's experiences are inclusive, positive and nurturing. However, additional support for children where SEBD have been identified is also needed to meet their individual needs and support their learning and development.

1. Curriculum planning

At setting level there needs to be a high standard of planning and evaluation to ensure that the curriculum is effective in supporting all children's learning. It is very important not to develop activities and then consider how these could be differentiated for children with SEBD after the fact. Curriculum development should take into account all children's needs from the start. Too often, children with learning difficulties find they are facing a 'bolt-on' approach to meeting their needs, or they are isolated in the session as they cannot access particular activities or they are removed from the session to do something else instead. Curriculum planning needs to be innovative, varied, based on children's progress to date and involving a balanced range of self-chosen and directed activities. For example, encouraging children to use a range of methods of recording or preparing feedback on a story, to suit their own needs, is very important where literacy levels vary widely. This encourages all children to join in when working on literacy skills and does not distinguish those with learning difficulties. Children can provide feedback orally, through pictures or drawings, in writing or through role play.

2. Monitoring and assessment

Observation of children with SEBD provides vital information to feed into planning and to assess the child's progress and level of ability. It also provides a basis for discussion with parents and other professionals on the relevance of support. Perhaps most importantly, observation provides an opportunity to debunk assumptions and stereotypes about a child based on partial under-standings of the issues he faces or disabilities he has. Good quality observation and analysis also provide the opportunity to focus on the child's strengths and abilities, rather than the more common deficit model. The Code of Practice cites observation as the basis for decision-making for a child with SEN, and monitoring of children with SEBD is vital to ensuring that the strategies which are in place to support them are effective. However, it is important to ensure that staff are skilled in a range of observation methods; that they understand the purposes of observations; and that they are able to effectively analyse observations to inform curriculum planning and support strategies. Two important approaches are sociograms, which track children's social interactions, and target-child observa-tions, which provide a detailed and in-depth account of a single child's behaviour and activities.

Are we getting it right?

Observations can also be used to explore whether a child's SEBD may be exacerbated by policies and practices in the setting, or by the attitudes and behaviour of practitioners. It is important that these factors are considered as part of the support process for the child and that it is recognized that children may develop SEBD, or these may become more pronounced, in response to policies and practices that do not effectively support devel-opment. Look at the questions below and, with colleagues or your mentor, discuss how you might find the answers to them in respect of children with SEBD in your workplace or placement:

◆ Are the children able to genuinely succeed in their activities?

◆ Is feedback constructive and genuine?

◆ Is the curriculum interesting and engaging?

◆ Are some children excluded from activities because of learning difficulties?

◆ Do some children have 'difficult' or 'behaviour-problem' labels?

◆ Is child development and diverse development well understood?

◆ Is the environment well managed and organized?

◆ Are there high expectations of all children according to their current level of ability?

◆ Are there mechanisms for reviewing practices and policy if they do not meet all children's needs?

◆ Is there an effective and positive behaviour management policy in practice?

3. Supporting self-esteem and social interactions

For many children, the main and most interesting aspect of being in a setting is the chance to make friends and interact with other children. Children who are experiencing social and emotional difficulties may find making friends very difficult and it is well documented that children with learning difficulties and/or behavioural problems are more likely to be socially rejected by peers. Social rejection can make time in the setting a distressing and negative experience and may impact on all aspects of development.

Responses are needed on several levels. Practitioners need to simultaneously support the development of positive self-esteem and children's access to play and social activities. Supporting self-esteem can be actieved by:

♦ ensuring opportunities to succeed

♦ practitioners role-modelling positive regard for the child to other children

♦ demonstrating high expectations and positive faith in the child

♦ dealing sensitively with behavioural problems (see below)

♦ targeting the child for genuine praise and rewards for progress

♦ finding out the child's strengths and focusing on these

♦ showing warmth and affection to the child

♦ whole-setting approaches to creating an ethos of respect and positive regard for all.

Behavioural, Emotional and Social Difficulties

Supporting children's access to social play and interactions with other children can include:

♦ discussing friendship, bullying and inclusion issues in circle time

♦ using stories to show the group how important including other children is

♦ showing friendship and positive regard for the child yourself

♦ playing with the child and inviting other children to join you

♦ joining existing play with the child

♦ highlighting the child's successes and areas of ability

♦ creating a 'circle of friends' for an isolated child

♦ pairing and grouping children to promote relationships

♦ being firm about issues of bullying and negative behaviour between children

♦ getting parents involved in anti-bullying strategies.

Sometimes children are left feeling unsuccessful and rejected because of a lack of consideration of particular issues, as the following example suggests:

Why isn't my child's work on the wall?

On parents' evening for Year 1, Dan's father went to school to see his teacher. While waiting for his

---

appointment time, he wandered the corridors of the school looking at the many displays of different types of work that covered the walls. Gradually he realized that not one piece of Dan's work was there. Dan's writing was unclear and his artwork tended to be messy and often not conforming to the activity brief. The teacher was appalled to discover that in choosing 'good' work to hang on the wall, Dan's work had been entirely excluded. This was rectified immediately and Dan's work appeared, reflecting his individualistic approach to art and his own ways of communicating his ideas and responses. How do you think Dan felt about this? What sort of work is displayed in your setting?

4. Meeting emotional needs

Porter (2003) defined children's emotional needs as:

♦ security

♦ self-esteem

♦ autonomy

♦ belonging

♦ fun

♦ self-expression.

Children need their emotional needs met in order to:

♦ develop maturity and confidence

♦ learn with confidence

- develop social skills, friendships and rewarding relationships
- regulate emotional responses
- respond to others' needs. (from Kay 2006: 119)

In order to create a positive environment for emotional development, a setting can:

- promote a secure environment with respect and caring as key elements
- help children with emotional problems to problem-solve through conversation, interventions, group discussion and 'what if?' scenarios
- use learning opportunities to develop confidence and autonomy
- maintain a calm, orderly environment with awareness of the additional needs of children suffering from stress generated elsewhere
- recognize that young children may find it difficult to manage strong feelings and emotions.

Specific interventions

Children with SEBD may need specific interventions to support their learning development and help them engage successfully in learning activities. Interventions need to be based on a clear understanding of the child's needs, and may be part of Early Years or School Action or Action Plus if other professionals are involved, or the child's statement. It is very important to tailor interventions to the child rather than try standard interventions without consideration of individual needs. In addition, interventions need to be monitored and evaluated to ensure they are effective. If interventions are not appropriate this may increase the child's difficulties and the child's SEBD may become more apparent. To summarize, interventions need to be:

♦ based on assessment of the child's needs, including the child's and parents' views, observations and records of the child's activities and progress and assessment by other professionals where appropriate

♦ focused on clear aims and targets

♦ responsive, well-thought out and 'matched' to the child's needs

♦ monitored and evaluated

♦ recorded

♦ developed or changed in response to outcomes.

Interventions may be part of a child's IEP, and as such should be reviewed regularly with other professionals, parents and the child's input.

1. Interventions within the setting

These could include working one-to-one with a practitioner to achieve particular targets or working in a group to develop social skills. They could involve building concentration through short, focused sessions on an activity, or encouraging play by playing with the child or alongside. Interventions can focus on social and play skills, learning or behaviour. For children with SEBD related to specific disabilities such as ADHD, this might involve establishing routines to support the child's concentration and giving the child a 'time out' location for when she is feeling under stress. It may involve using visual images to support the child's understanding of what is expected, such as labels on play materials and on other resources. It is important that children with SEBD do not have all their interventions outside the group. They need to share their activities with other children to build social skills. However, children who have SEBD due to ASDs may need more 'quiet' time than others, and children with anger-management problems or high levels of anxiety may also need time away from the group. There are a number of specific strategies to use with autistic children which can be found at the National Autistic Society website (www.nas.org.uk) and on the Teachernet site at (www.teachernet.gov.uk). Behaviour-management strategies are discussed in more detail below.

In any intervention, the child needs to know what is expected and what the intervention is aimed at achieving. Appropriate praise should be given for progress.

2. Interventions involving other professionals

These could involve physiotherapy to support physical skills; speech and language therapy; or work with specialist support teams around language, visual or hearing impairments. For many, assessment and advice on interventions may be part of the role of advisory teachers and educational psychologists. Other professionals become involved when a child is in need of support services beyond the capacity of the setting. These may include interventions that do not focus directly on the child, for example supporting parenting improvements through parenting programmes. Children's centres are likely to offer parenting programmes as part of integrated service delivery, but for parents of children attending other early years settings these may be accessed through family support services or health services. Other interventions may include social services supporting children in need or at risk of abuse. There are also voluntary sector organizations that may offer services outside the setting, such as the Dyslexia Institute which offers tuition directly to children with dyslexia.

Behaviour support

Whole-settings approaches

Supporting individual children's behavioural development needs to take place within whole-setting approaches which create supportive environments for children. Using this type of approach, individual behaviour management is only part of a wider strategy. Settings can 'prevent and minimize' unwanted behaviour through a range of approaches and in this way create environments that may help children's behavioural development and which will reduce behavioural problems. As discussed earlier, children with SEBD may find themselves in a negative spiral if factors in the setting reinforce behavioural problems and poor levels of learning support exacerbate emotional stress and social difficulties.

Key features of whole-settings approaches are:

♦ clear and well-publicized behavioural standards that are culturally sensitive and negotiated with practitioners, parents and children

♦ open discussion and negotiation with children about expected behavioural standards within which their input is respected and responded to, e.g. through circle time and school council

♦ open discussion with parents about behavioural standards

♦ support for parents and information sharing between parents and practitioners on behavioural standards and management

♦ regular discussion within the setting to ensure behaviour policy is followed and issues about behaviour are shared.

Other factors relate to recommendations made within the Ofsted report *Managing Challenging Behaviour* (March 2005). These include:

♦ improving the quality of teaching and providing a curriculum which engages children and meets their needs

♦ supporting the literacy and communication skills of children with behavioural problems

♦ good systems for tracking academic and social development, used to improve children's behaviour

♦ training for practitioners at all levels in behaviour management and child development

♦ reviewing ways of making links with parents

♦ reinforcing consistent approaches within the setting.

A key factor in this is ensuring that all children can access the curriculum. For many children, behavioural problems are closely associated with the frustration and humiliation of not being able to manage learning activities.

Establishing an effective whole-setting policy relies on high-quality leadership; training; parent partnership; and effective assessment and support for children's individual needs.

Practitioner behaviour and attitudes

Practitioners have a responsibility to be good role models for children's behaviour through considering the impact of their own behaviour on the individual child and group. Shouting is a clear example of this. Although some practitioners maintain that shouting is required to keep group under control, there are many others who have good control without raising their voices. Shouting offers children a model of negative behaviour and promotes their shouting, too. It may be very distressing to some children, especially those on the autistic spectrum who are noise-sensitive, and it may produce aggressive behaviour in some children. For other children, shouting may reflect domestic or child abuse in the home. Practitioners need to role model:

♦ respectful and courteous behaviour

♦ good communication

♦ avoidance of shouting, angry expressions or power-assertion

♦ positive statements and attitudes to others

♦ empathy and sensitivity towards others' needs

♦ helpfulness and supportive behaviour

♦ equity and fairness. (Kay 2006: 110)

Practitioners need support to achieve these standards through training and development opportunities, mentoring and supervision of new staff and regular discussion about behaviour management strategies.

Practitioners also need good curriculum planning and delivery skills to ensure children are engaged and capable of managing and benefiting from activities and tasks. Verbal interactions with children are central to extending learning and thinking and practitioners need to be skilled in communicating with children. Other skills and abilities include:

- good knowledge of the curriculum
- good understanding of child development
- formative feedback
- balancing child-initiated and adult initiated play and activities
- effective behaviour management strategies
- ability to create accessible environments with play space, quiet space, easy access to storage, good movement flows and flexibility in usage.

EPPE (2003) findings included the following negative practices:

- no follow-up on behavioural issues
- behaviour is dealt with by telling children to stop
- distraction is seen as a strategy for managing behaviour.

Behavioural issues need to be dealt with within a wider strategy and not as isolated incidents.

Managing individual behaviour

Key factors to consider when responding to behavioural incidents are:

- what you know about the child's circumstances, needs, situation and abilities/disabilities
- the child's character and personality

Behavioural, Emotional and Social Difficulties

◆ the context of the behaviour and whether other children were involved

◆ whether the behaviour is part of a pattern or not

◆ the severity of concern about the behaviour

◆ whether the behaviour caused a risk to the child, other children or adults.

Principles which need to underpin any response are:

◆ the safety of all children and adults

◆ any short-term response to the incident needs to be followed up with a longer-term strategy

◆ it is not about winning or losing

◆ the child's self-esteem must not be damaged

◆ the aim is to promote positive behaviour

◆ individual behaviour management needs to take place within whole-setting policy and strategies around behaviour management.

Possible responses could include:

◆ reminding the child of rules/boundaries and expectations

◆ supporting the child to cope with mistakes through sensitive interventions

◆ helping the child who is struggling

♦ stopping sequences of behaviour at an early stage by intervening, moving the child, changing the focus of attention, sitting with the child

♦ being responsive to the child who is seeking attention through behaviour

♦ giving the child 'quiet space' to calm down in.

Practitioners need to remain calm and objective during behavioural incidents and to be assertive with the child and clear about what they want him to do. It is important also to acknowledge the child's feelings and to be problem-solving in one's approach, looking for ways to support the child in resolving the issue. Young children can be very distressed by their own outbursts and may need a warm and comforting approach in order to calm down. The child needs to be reminded of behavioural expectations but not at length.

Chronic and repeated negative patterns of behaviour can result in the child being seen negatively by adults and children and this may lead to social isolation and 'labelling' the child as a problem to be solved. Strategies to deal with persistent behavioural problems should include:

♦ target-setting through the child's IEP

♦ seeking support from other professionals and agencies

♦ working with parents

♦ ensuring the child's needs are fully understood through relevant assessment and monitoring

- working as a team and providing a consistent response
- changing strategies that do not help the child
- ensuring the strategy includes ways of helping the child improve his behaviour and not just ways of containing it
- taking time to reflect on aspects of the curriculum and environment which may not support the child's improvement
- avoiding seeing the child in a negative light, and ensuring any practitioner who is becoming exhausted and fatalistic about a child is supported.

Behavioural incidents should always be reflected on to ensure that practitioners have a good understanding of their own behaviour and how to best support the child.

Jamie, 4 years old

Jamie was identified as having SEBD after entering foster care at the age of 3 and starting nursery. His challenging behaviour had been highlighted as one of the reasons why his mother had not been able to continue to care for Jamie. It was clear from his records that he had not been given boundaries in his birth home and that difficult behaviour had been 'rewarded' with attention from his mother, which was otherwise at a low level. Jamie was insecurely attached to his mother and had become distraught since coming into care. In nursery and at his foster home, Jamie's behaviour was very difficult to manage. He spat, kicked, shouted and swore at staff and children, threw toys and other objects at them and laughed at practitioners who tried to stop him doing these things. One young nursery nurse was heard to say at lunchtime that she 'hated' Jamie and could not bear to be in a room with him. A more experienced colleague explained that Jamie had not received the love and attention he needed from his mother from birth and he did not know his father. This had left him feeling insecure and sometimes abandoned. He had discovered that being 'naughty' got his mother's attention and continued to use this approach as it had worked for him in the past. Separation from his mother had left Jamie feeling anxious, angry and confused. His self-esteem and sense of belonging were very poor. He felt unloved and 'different' from other children who lived with their birth parents. He thought something was wrong with him and this is why his mother had given him up. At 4, this was a lot to bear and Jamie found day-to-day situations hard to cope with. Jamie deserved the compassion and support of practitioners and their understanding and affection.

Conclusion

In this chapter, some of the approaches to supporting children with SEBD have been discussed, with emphasis on whole-setting approaches and preventative strategies. Key factors identified are high-quality pedagogies, warm relationships and coherent strategies for behaviour management.

5

Working in Partnership

In this chapter, the role of partnerships between professionals and agencies and parents will be explored within the framework of support discussed in Chapter 3. Strategies and policies for partnership development will be discussed as will the role of the practitioner in working with others. Types of partnerships will be considered, as will barriers to effective partnership and strategies to overcome these.

The learning outcomes from this chapter include:

♦ understanding the value of working in partnership with other professionals and agencies and parents

♦ understanding the role and contribution of key professional partners

♦ exploring strategies for effective partnership development and the individual practitioner's role within these

♦ understanding the barriers to effective partnership working and how these can be addressed.

The purpose of partnership between professionals and agencies

Children with SEBD often need and receive services from a range of agencies, supporting different aspects of their development. These can include early years settings and schools, health services, social services, local authority SEN services and, possibly, voluntary sector agencies. In order for children's needs to be met, professionals must provide services that are coordinated, complementary and effective, and which cover all aspects of needs. Traditional divides between different aspects of service delivery mean that children and families have in the past (and still sometimes are) disadvantaged by poorly coordinated, inefficient and contradictory service delivery. Partnership between professionals and agencies in service planning and delivery has been demonstrated to be positive for children, parents and practitioners and is now enshrined within legislation and policy affecting children of all ages. Recent moves to further integrate service delivery are being driven by the Every Child Matters agenda discussed in Chapter 3.

Behaviour and educational support teams (BESTs): an example of partnership working

BESTs were introduced between 2002 and 2006 in targeted LAs as part of the DfES Behaviour Improvement Programme (BiP), which had an overall aim of reducing behavioural problems and increasing attendance in the target schools. Targeted schools had a high number of exclusions and poor attendance, indicating a high number of pupils who would or had developed behavioural problems. BESTs are multi-agency teams, often based in a secondary school but serving a cluster of secondary and primary schools. There are 1,700 primary schools involved with a BEST, which was aimed at supporting children aged 5–18 years. Their focus was supporting schools and individual children with EBD or likely to develop EBD to help with early identification and intervention in order to improve behaviour and attendance and children's overall well-being (Behaviour Improvement Programme, DfES 2006a). The teams included health, social work and education professionals, including educational welfare officers and Child and Adolescent Mental Health (CAMHS) workers.

The National Foundation for Educational Research (NFER) evaluation of the BESTs found that:

♦ the majority worked mainly with individual children and families

♦ other work included groupwork and whole-school interventions

♦ groupwork included circle time and parent-support groups as the most common approaches

♦ whole-school approaches focused mainly on supporting schools to develop behaviour management strategies. (Halsey *et al.* 2006)

The outcomes of the BESTs included improvements in attainment, attendance, behaviour and wellbeing. These improvements were alluded to as a 'hierarchy' with good levels of child and family wellbeing as the basis for effective interventions to improve attendance and behaviour and better attainment as the final outcome.

Parents benefited through:

♦ improved access to services

♦ more effective/re-establishment of home–school links

♦ improved parenting.

School staff benefited from:

♦ improved strategies and better skills for managing behaviour and emotional difficulties

♦ improved access to specialist support services

♦ increased understanding of EBD

♦ a better ability to support pupils.

Other agencies benefited through:

♦ less pressure on workload/referrals

♦ better relationships with schools and families

♦ better access to children and families needing services.

Factors that supported BEST effectiveness were:

♦ the development of multi-agency teams with professionals sharing expertise and skills and developing a more holistic approach to working with children and families through this process

♦ co-location in either school, community or LA premises to facilitate team cohesion and develop identity as a service

♦ accessibility to schools and families, including easier referrals and meetings in home or school

♦ good levels of communication between schools and BESTs, e.g. regular planning and review meetings, a key contact in school

♦ positive and regular communication within the team linked to the development of a multi-agency ethos, sharing information and blurring professional boundaries

♦ development of a holistic approach to children's needs, including working with parent's issues. (Halsey *et al.* 2006)

BESTs highlight the fact that school-based initiatives need to involve other professionals with a range of skills, as educational approaches alone may not help children with key issues affecting their development.

Developing partnership between professionals

There are different degrees of partnership, which has led to a plethora of terms to describe relationships between agencies and professionals. Key terms for the purpose of this discussion are:

♦ Interdisciplinary working: where professionals and agencies work in cooperation with each other within agreed strategies and protocols, but essentially remain working within their own agencies.

♦ Integrated services: where professionals from different disciplines work together within the same setting or agency.

Most practitioners currently deliver services within an interdisciplinary framework, although integrated services are increasing and include the development of children's centres and extended schools. However, within current policy, practitioners are generally working regularly with other professionals in some capacity to support children with SEN. Despite the policy thrust towards integrated service delivery, considerable difficulties can lie in the way of effective partnership. These may include:

♦ failure to understand or value other professionals' roles

♦ blame cultures and traditional enmities

♦ poor communication

♦ different plans, aims and goals

♦ different perspectives on children and families

♦ different theoretical or disciplinary frameworks.

In order to develop effective partnerships, practitioners need to develop skills in working with others from different professional backgrounds, understandings of children and professional goals.

Key skills and knowledge for effective partnership working include:

♦ understanding the roles and responsibilities of professional partners

♦ sharing understandings and information about the child

♦ developing joint plans and delivery strategies and making joint decisions

♦ viewing the child's needs holistically

♦ developing effective communication between partners

♦ developing an ethos in which partnership working is welcome and sought after

♦ sharing expertise and ideas

♦ developing a joint working culture.

Activity

List the professionals you have worked with in supporting children with SEBD. Describe their primary roles and responsibilities and check your understandings of these with a colleague or mentor.

Structures which support partnership working between professionals and agencies working with children with SEN include:

◆ policy and legislative frameworks which promote partnership, e.g. Code of Practice

◆ the integration of LAs and children's social services into Children's Service Authorities

◆ joint commissioning and funding of some services through Children's Trusts

◆ the development of the Common Assessment Framework

◆ joint planning structures for individual children, e.g. interdisciplinary reviews

◆ the central coordinating role of the SENCO.

Brenda, 3 years old

Brenda has been in your setting for 3 months and is displaying some difficult behaviour and emotional distress. She has global developmental delays and does not willingly play or interact with other children. You have discussed Brenda with the SENCO in the setting and agreed that further assessment needs to take place to support Brenda. However, attempts to engage her mother in discussion about Brenda's needs have been greeted with suspicion. A social worker has now contacted you to say that there is a child protection investigation taking place after neighbours reported that Brenda was left alone for long periods and that her mother has a drug abuse problem.

> What steps need to be taken to ensure there is
> a coordinated response to the child and mother's
> needs? Which other professionals should be
> involved?

Managers have a central responsibility to ensure
that interdisciplinary working is part of whole-setting
development and that the setting has strategies for
improving partnership working. These could include:

♦ accessing joint training where possible

♦ making links with key professionals and developing
  relationships

♦ ensuring arrangements for meetings and planning
  are accessible to all partners

♦ developing an ethos where working with others is
  valued and promoted.

Partnership with parents

Partnership with parents has been a key element of policy
in the early years, and is supported by research evidence
that demonstrates the value of such partnerships for
children, parents and practitioners. However, there is
also evidence that partnership with parents can remain
elusive with some parents described as 'hard to reach',
and with partnerships that remain unequal in terms of
power distribution between parents and practitioners.

Many parents are involved with settings, but
involvement may not be the same as partnership

and may vary significantly between settings and parents. For example, one primary school prided itself on a high level of parent partnership but on closer evaluation discovered that a small group of the same parents, mainly white women, were involved in fundraising, governors and parent meetings and helping out in school. Men, and parents from ethnic minority backgrounds were conspicuous by their absence and some parents had never entered the school gates.

Developing partnership with parents

Partnership with parents with children with SEBD may be subject to issues and difficulties over and above the difficulties of engaging with other parents. Parents with children with SEBD may be struggling with social isolation and economic hardship. They may have parenting problems that impact negatively on their ability to enjoy parenting. They may have difficulties dealing with their child's behavioural problems or feel negatively about their child being identified as having SEN. It is possible that some parents may feel anxious or hostile towards educational or 'authority' figures or bewildered about the jargon and systems associated with SEN. Parents of children with disabilities may be exhausted and distressed by their child's diagnosis, worried about the future and unsure of what to expect. The outcome may be that parents do not always present at their best and may be hostile, angry, upset or withdrawn from the processes surrounding their child. Factors affecting parent involvement can include:

♦ negative views of education based on their own experiences

♦ the impact of social isolation, poverty and lack of resources on parents' ability to cope and self-esteem

♦ concerns about being blamed for their child's problems

♦ lack of time, transport, childcare for other children

♦ alienation in the professional group in terms of understanding language, jargon and issues

♦ lack of clear information about their child's issues, support mechanisms, other services.

Sara, 24 years old

Sara left school at 15 after years of truancy and difficult behaviour in school. Sara remembers her school days as 'torture', feeling constantly humiliated by her poverty, slow learning and lack of friends. Sara had Malcolm after a brief relationship and is now raising him alone. After social workers became involved when there were concerns about Malcolm's care, Sara sent him to nursery on their recommendation. She didn't feel she had a lot of choice about this. The social worker has also arranged for paediatric assessment as she thinks Malcolm is too withdrawn and uncommunicative, and that he may have ASD.

At nursery, Sara drops Malcolm off in the minimum time possible and does not talk to the practitioners. Attempts at home visiting before Malcolm started nursery were unsuccessful.

Malcolm's key worker waited with him one day and before Sara could grab him and disappear, he told Sara about how well Malcolm had worked on a painting activity that day. The practitioner then showed Sara the painting and asked her what Malcolm liked to do at home. Gradually, over the next few weeks, the practitioner made regular efforts to talk to Sara and build a relationship. Finally, he asked Sara what she did when Malcolm turned his back on her and refused to engage. At this point, Sara poured out her worries and fears about Malcolm and, for the first time, she and the practitioner shared their strategies for helping Malcolm.

In order to develop effective partnerships with parents, several factors need to be borne in mind:

♦ parents hold the most information about all aspects of their child's development

♦ parents should be treated with respect and supported to understand the issues affecting their child

♦ parents should be given maximum help to access meetings and other opportunities to discuss their child

♦ if parents seem reluctant to engage then practitioners need to think of different approaches to involve them

♦ parents' concerns, feelings, wishes and worries need to be listened to carefully and responded to.

Practitioners and settings can support parents by:

♦ ensuring that meetings are held at times parents can attend

♦ giving parents information regularly and checking that this is understood

♦ supporting parents to make contributions to their child's IEP reviews and service planning

♦ developing relationships with parents by showing warmth and concern and respecting their views

♦ acknowledging parents' concerns

♦ acknowledging parents' roles in supporting their children

♦ advocating for parents with other professionals

♦ making sure parents are aware of parent partnership services through the local authority and other support groups

♦ ensuring parents have access to parenting and family support as required

♦ communicating in ways that support parents' understandings.

Partnerships with parents should be supported through SEN policies and parent partnership policies which emphasize positive aspects of building relationships, and which have been developed with parents and made available to them.

The whole-setting context

Partnership with parents of children with SEBD needs to take place in the context of wider partnership development within the setting. Parents need to be involved with the setting at all levels if partnership is to be successful, and strategies to involve all parents need to take into account that they are not a homogenous group, but diverse in their interests, abilities, views and opinions. As such, the most successful partnerships are built through flexible and variable ways of involving parents, including:

♦ home-visiting

♦ induction and transition meetings

♦ regular information sharing through newsletters, noticeboards, informal discussion, formal meetings

♦ easy access to the setting, a warm welcome and good communication channels

♦ confidentiality and respect for information shared

♦ a range of methods for giving parents regular feedback about their child

♦ information sharing about other sources of support

♦ involving parents in planning and delivering the curriculum, including using parents' skills respectfully.

It is also important to be sure that if partnerships are failing to develop that there may be other more effective approaches to developing these.

Conclusion

Partnerships with other professionals and parents are key in supporting and planning for children with SEBD. However, partnerships involve effort and consideration and barriers exist to developing them successfully. Settings need to have structures and policies to support partnerships in line with current national policy and legislation, and practitioners need to be supported to develop skills in building relationships to promote partnership.

Conclusion

Early identification and support for young children with behavioural, social and emotional SEN is vital to ensuring that they have the maximum access to learning and other developmental opportunities. Practitioners in early years settings are ideally placed to identify children with SEBD and to provide this support in partnership with parents and other professionals. However, in order to be effective in this role, practitioners need to have a clear understanding of the influences on children's social, emotional and behavioural development and the complex causes of difficulties in these areas. They also need to have knowledge of the policy and legislative framework in which work with children with SEN takes place and approaches to supporting children's social, emotional and behavioural development.

This book gives a starting point to any practitioner working with children with SEBD. It tries to promote a developmental approach to supporting children, and the positive aspects of partnership. The book also emphasizes the need to understand the individual child's background, needs and experiences in order to provide appropriate support. Finally, the book encourages practitioners to continue to learn about and reflect on their own practice in this area and to keep apace of policy and practice developments through their own research and contact with others.

References

Ainsworth, M. D. S., Blehar, M. C., Waters, E. and Wall, S. (1978); *Patterns of Attachment*. Hillsdale, NJ: Erlbaum.

Audit Commission (2002), *Special Educational Needs: a Mainstream Issue*. www.audit-commission. gov.uk/reports/NATIONAL-REPORT.asp?Category ID=&ProdID=D3265D20_FD7D–11d6–B211–006008 5F8572&SectionID=sec1# (accessed January 2007).

Baumrind, D. (1967), 'Child care practices anteceding three patterns of pre-school behaviour', *Genetic Psychology Monographs*, 75, pp. 43–88.

Baumrind, D. (1973), 'The development of instrumental competence through socialization', in Pick, A. E. (ed.), *Minnesota Symposium on Child Psychology*. Minneapolis: University of Minneapolis Press, pp. 3–46.

Bee, H. (2000), *The Developing Child* (9th edition). Needham Heights, MA: Allyn and Bacon.

Belsky, J. (1984), 'The determinants of parenting: a process model', *Child Development*, 55, pp. 83–96.

Benner, G. J., Nelson, J. R., Epstein, M. H. (2002), 'Language skills of children with EBD: a literature review', *Journal of Emotional and Behavioural Disorders*, 10, (1), pp. 43–59.

Berger, A. (2006), 'Communication and behaviour: exploring the link'. Presentation at the ICAN conference 2006. www.ican.org.uk/upload/training/ann per cent20berger.pdf (accessed September 2006).

Bronfenbrenner, U. (1979), *The Ecology of Human Development*. Cambridge, MA: Harvard University Press.

Dekovic, M. and Janssens, J. M. A. M. (1992), 'Parents' child-rearing style and child's sociometric status', *Developmental Psychology*, 28, pp. 925–32.

Department for Education (DfE) (1994), *Code of Practice for the Identification and Assessment of Special Educational Needs*. London: HMSO

Department for Education and Skills (DfES) (2001), *Special Education Needs Code of Practice*. Nottingham: DfES Publications.

Department for Education and Skills (DfES) (2003), *Every Child Matters*. London: The Stationery Office.

Department for Education and Skills (DfES) (2004), *Removing Barriers to Achievement: The Government's Strategy for SEN*. London: DfES Publications.

Department for Education and Skills (DfES) (2006a), *Behaviour Improvement Programme (BIP)*. www.dfes.gov.uk/behaviourimprovement (accessed August 2006).

Department for Education and Skills (DfES) (2006b), *Early Support*. www.earlysupport.org.uk (accessed September 2006).

Department for Education and Skills (DfES) (2006c), *Quality Protects Work programme: Education issues*. www.dfes.gov.uk/qualityprotects/work_pro/project_8.shtml (accessed August 2006).

Department of Health (DoH) (2003), *Together from the Start: Practical guidance for professionals working with disabled children (birth to third birthday) and their families.* London: DoH Publications.

Department of Health (DoH) (2004), *National Service Framework for Children, Young People and Maternity Services.* London: DoH Publications.

Directgov (2006), *Support for Special Educational Needs: Parent partnership services and other organisations.* http://www.direct.gov.uk/EducationAndLearning/Schools/SpecialEducationalNeeds/Special EducationalNeedsArticles/fs/en?CONTENT_ ID=10016184&chk=guktPb (accessed August 2006).

Dyson, A. and Millward, A. (2000), 'SENCOs as decision-makers'. Presented at the International Special Education Congress, July 2000. www. isec2000.org.uk/abstracts/papers_d/dyson_1.htm (accessed July 2006).

EPPI (2003), *Supporting Pupils with Emotional and Behavioural Difficulties (EBD) in Mainstream Primary Schools: A systematic review of recent research on strategy effectiveness* (1999 to 2002). http://eppi. ioe.ac.uk/EPPIWeb/home.aspx?page=/reel/review_ groups/TTA/BM(IOE)/BM(IOE)_intro.htm (accessed July 2006).

Farroni, T., Johnson, M. H., Menon, E., Zulian, L., Faraguna, D., and Csibra, G. (2005), 'Newborns' preference for face-relevant stimuli: Effects of contrast polarity', 11 November, *PNAS*, (10.1073/pnas.0502205102).

Foot, H., Woolfson, L., Terras, M. and Norfolk, C. (2004), 'Handling hard-to-manage behaviours in pre-school provision: A systems approach', *Journal of Early Childhood Research*, 2 (2), pp. 111–38.

Foundation for People with Learning Disabilities (2006), *Young People with Learning Disabilities and Mental Health Problems*. www.learningdisabilities.org.uk/page.cfm?pageurl=count_us_in_background.cfm (accessed July 2006).

Ghate, D. and Hazel, N. (2002), *Parenting in Poor Environments: Stress, support and coping*. London: Jessica Kingsley Publishers.

Halsey, K., Gulliver, C., Johnson, A., Martin, K. and Kinder, K. (2006), *Evaluation of Behaviour and Education Support Teams*. London: DfES Publications.

Hargraves, D., Hester, S. and Mellor, F. (1975), *Deviance in Classrooms*. London: Routledge and Keegan Paul.

Jones, P. (2005), *Inclusion in the Early Years: Stories of good practice*. London: David Fulton.

Kay, J. (2006), *Managing Behaviour in the Early Years*. London: Continuum.

Laevers, F. (2003), 'Experiential education: Making care and education more effective through well-being and involvement', in Laevers, F. and Heylen, L. (eds), *Involvement of Children and Teacher Style: Insights from an international study on experiential education*. Studia Pedagogica, 35. Leuven: Leuven University Press, pp. 13–24.

Lewis, M. (2002), *Social Development*, in Slater, A. and Lewis, M. (eds), *Introduction to Infant Development*. Oxford: Oxford University Press.

Lindsay, G. Pather, S. and Strand, S. (2006), 'Special educational needs and ethnicity: Issues of over- and under-representation', research report (RR757) Annesley. Nottingham: DfES Publications. www.dfes.gov.uk/research/data/uploadfiles/RR757.pdf (accessed January 2007).

References

Maccoby, E. E., and Martin, J. A. (1983), 'Socialization in the context of the family: Parent–child inter-action', in P. H. Mussen (ed.) and E. M. Hetherington (vol. ed.), *Handbook of child psychology: Vol. 4. Socialization, personality, and social development* (4th edition), pp. 1–101. New York: Wiley.

MIND (2006), *Children and Young People and Mental Health*. www.mind.org.uk/NR/exeres/46D79426-BC46-4033-9DB2-C976664A11BB.htm?NRMODE=Published&wbc_purpose=Basic&WBCMODE=PresentationUnpublished# Statistics (accessed July 2006).

Mir, G., Nocon, A. and Ahmad, W. with Jones, L. (2001), *Learning Difficulties and Ethnicity* (Report to the Department of Health). London: DoH Publications.

Moffit, T. E. (1993), 'The neuropsychology of conduct disorder' *Development and Psychopathology*, 5 (2), pp. 135–52.

Norwich, B. and Kelly, N. A. A. (2006), 'Evaluating children's participation in SEN procedures: Lessons for educational psychologists', *Educational Psychology in Practice*, pp. 255–72.

NSPCC (2006), *Facts and Figures about Child Abuse*. www.nspcc.org.uk/home/newsandcampaigns/factsandfigures.htm (accessed August 2006).

Ofsted (March 2005), *Managing Challenging Behaviour*. www.Ofsted.gov.uk/publication/index/cfm?fuseaction=publications.displayfile&id=3846&type=pdf (accessed August 2006).

Patterson, G. R. (1996), 'Some characteristics of a developmental theory for early-onset juvenile delin-quency', in M. F. Lenzenweger and J. J. Haugaard (eds), *Frontiers of Developmental Psychopathology* pp. 81–124. New York: Oxford University Press.

Pierce, E., Ewing, L. and Campbell, S. (1999), 'Diagnostic status and symptomatic behaviour of hard-to-manage preschool children I middle childhood and early adolescence', *Journal of Clinical Child Psychology*, 28 (10), pp. 44–57.

Porter, L. (2002), 'Emotional and social needs', in Porter, L. (ed.), *Educating Young Children with Special Needs.* London: Paul Chapman.

Porter, L. (2003), *Young Children's Behaviour: Practical approaches for caregivers and teachers* (2nd edition). London: Paul Chapman.

Ramsey, J. L. and Langlois, J. H. (2002), 'Effects of the "beauty is good" stereotype on children's information processing', *Journal of Experimental Child Psychology*, 81, pp. 320–40.

Roffey, S. (2004), *The New Teacher's Survival Guide to Behaviour*, London: Paul Chapman Publishing.

Rogers, B. (2000), *Behaviour Management: A whole school approach.* London: Paul Chapman Publishing.

Rogers, R., Tod, J., Powell, S., Parsons, C., Godfrey, R., Graham-Matheson, L., Carlson, A. and Cornwall, J. (2006), *Evaluation of Special Educational Needs Parent Partnership Services in England.* Notts.: DfEs Publications, Canterbury Christ Church University College.

Sammons, P., Sylva, K., Melhuish, E. C., Siraj-Blatchford, I., Taggart, B. and Elliot, K. (2002), *The Effective Provision of Pre-School Education (EPPE) Project: Technical Paper 8b: Measuring the impact of pre-school on children's social/behavioural development*

References

over the pre-school period. London: DfES/Institute of Education, University of London.

Schopler, E. (1995), *Parent Survival Manual: A guide to crisis resolution in autism and related disorders*. New York and London: Plenum Press.

Skidmore, D. (2004), *Inclusion: The dynamic of school development*. Buckingham: Open University Press.

Smith, P. K., Cowie, H. and Blades, M. (1998), *Understanding Children's Development* (3rd edition). Oxford: Blackwell Publishers.

Teachernet (2006), 'Removing barriers to acheivement'. www.teachernet.gov.uk/wholeschool/sen/senstrategy/ (accessed August 2006).

Utting, W. (1997), *People Like Us: The report of the review of the safeguards for children living away from home*. London: HMSO.

Weare, K. (2004,) *Developing the Emotionally Literate School*. London: Paul Chapman.

Williams, D., Goldstein, G. and Minshew, N. J. (2006), 'Neuropsychologic functioning in children with autism: Further evidence for disordered complex information-processing', *Child Neuropsychology*, 12 (4–5), pp. 279–98.